Copyright 1999 by Holistic Management International

Library of Congress Cataloguing-in-Publication
ISBN 978-0-9673941-0-7

Illustrations by Jane Reed and Marce Rackstraw
Design by Anne Tyler
Cover Design by Marisa Mancini

dedication

There comes a time in most people's lives when they are confronted with the depth of their longing for a deep sense of community, family, meaning, contribution, or some other value. This book is for those who have had the courage to look more deeply at that longing instead of turning their backs and seeking refuge in the daily business of survival.

A vision without a task

is but a dream.

A task without a vision

is drudgery.

A vision and a task

is the hope of the world

—Found in a church in Essex, England

acknowledgments

My first thanks goes to all the people who contributed stories and shared their lives with strangers to make this book far more lively and inviting than it would have been without their examples. I would also like to thank my editing cast of thousands who made this book clearer every time I thought I was done, particularly Preston Sullivan, Cindy Dvergsten, Larry Johnson, and Jim Parker. Special thanks goes to Jody Butterfield who, like a terrier with a bone, wouldn't let go of her conviction that I could produce a better draft than the one I had just handed her. Additional thanks to Anne Tyler, not only for her incredible ability to spot a typographical error, but also for her design and layout skills that transformed an interesting text into a work of art. Thanks also to Marce Rackstraw and Jane Reed for bringing alive my ideas with their illustrations. Lastly, I would like to thank my family, particularly Bonnie and Ben, for providing me with a wealth of information, putting up with me dragging this manuscript everywhere, and talking incessantly about this book. I couldn't have asked for a more willing and able crew.

table of contents

Seasoned Travelers

In the past, I virtually closed the door on any opportunity to access significant financial resources because I thought that, by definition, they would mean I had to sell out. In my upbringing, doing humanitarian work (serving God through serving others) was emphasized, and salary levels and nest-egg goals were downplayed. So I had deliberately chosen to limit myself to low-paying jobs.

Holistic Management helped me understand that having a high-paying job could be an avenue to accomplish other, non-money-oriented objectives. It was only a few weeks after my first workshop in Holistic Management that I had the opportunity to move into a new career area and enter a higher income level. That workshop was instrumental in my evaluation of options, and feeling absolutely certain about my decision. That job was a stepping-stone that led to my recent move into another significantly higher salaried position. Again, I reviewed my holisticgoal and was able to easily see how these changes would bring me more of the things I truly value in life, in my workplace, as well as in my relationship with family/friends and with the land I love in the New Mexico mountains.

The process and the structure of Holistic Management have decreased my anxiety in decision-making, and freed me up to make choices that I know will move me closer to achieving well-rounded, ethical and intentional life goals. As a result, I feel more balanced, confident, and full of gratitude.

Roci Galyn

Software Training Program Manager
Centerville, Virginia

When I choose to tell a story about how Holistic Management has affected our family, I tell the story of the change in my father. When I was growing up, I saw a young man making huge decisions and trying to meet the goals that he and his father established. I saw someone who was frustrated by the people that worked for him because none of them could or would work as hard as he did to make his dream come true. As I became an adult and started making my own life decisions, I figured there had to be a better way to live life.

When Holistic Management came into my father's life and he really started studying it, I saw him relax a little. I think he finally felt that everything wasn't sitting on his shoulders alone. As we all made the decision to come back to the ranch, he has learned to share with us the responsibility for making decisions and to communicate with us when needed. He is a lot more comfortable to be around and a calmer person. We all have a lot of growing to do in our understanding and practice of Holistic Management, but I think my father has done an admirable job of breaking old paradigms of thought and learning.

Jennifer Wheeling
Durango, Colorado

I have realized that the most significant aspect of this approach [Holistic Management] to life is how it has helped me see the abundance I experience in life as opposed to the deficits. The budget we created budgeted in money for me to spend on clothes and recreation (for fun things, and things the word "budget" had not included in my mind in the past). My diet showed me how to feed my body, not starve it, and the choices my family makes with our holistic-goal in mind keeps us focused on what we can have, as opposed to what we cannot. For someone like me, who heard "we can't afford that" and "No, you can't buy that" all my life, this made living with a budget far more palatable and manageable.

Bonnie Smith

University Program Manager of Services for the Deaf and Hard of Hearing
Albuquerque, New Mexico

As a family, we have a common desire to live in harmony with each other and to keep the land in our trust as open space and a home for our extended family. To do this takes a great deal of unselfish courage. Holistic Management helps each member of our family overcome and rise above the challenges of false pride, selfishness, impatience, self-pity, self-righteousness, etc. These are challenges everyone has to face any place they are and whatever their job, but the demand to express patience, unselfish love, joy, humility and respect is doubled when you live near and work with other family members. The reward is, however, that as we get better and better at expressing those positive living qualities, we are making a better "climate" for our family, our community, and our world. In our mind, we might as well expend that kind of effort because there is nothing to be lost and everything to be gained!

Kay James

Co-owner of James Ranch
Durango, Colorado

preface

who is this book for?

This book is specifically for families (households) who have just learned about Holistic Management®*, but who want more guidance in this process. While anyone can use this information about Holistic Management, this publication specifically addresses family/household issues and interests.

For those people who would like more detailed information than this text provides, Appendix 2 lists additional resources. If you have questions that arise as you read this book, please refer to the other publications mentioned in Appendix 2 or contact Holistic Management International for more information about how to receive training.

why read this book?

The point of this book is to help people understand the Holistic Management process and how they can use it to create the life they want. Regardless of how you define a better or more meaningful life, you can use your desire for it as a springboard for learning the Holistic Management process. In turn, you will determine what and how you can contribute to the world around you which will bring more meaning to your life.

So what I offer here is an explanation of a process many families, couples, individuals, businesses, and communities have found helpful. It is a process by which we can determine what moves us or what is of great importance to us, then make decisions, and take ongoing action to help us create the life we want. That might not seem like such a revolutionary act, but as you'll read in the stories ahead, it has had some dramatic results for many people.

As you begin reading this book, think about the ways you can engage the important people in your life as you learn and integrate this process. Throughout the book, there are stories and exercises that will help you engage others and keep up the momentum you will create, but the sooner you can elicit support for your effort, the more you will get from the beginning exercises. While this process can be used by individuals, those of us who have incorporated Holistic Management into our lives have found that it is more productive and fun to work in a group so that each of us can support one another in our evolutions. This is true of a couple, a family, a

---

* Holistic Management® is a trademark of the Holistic Management International

small-business owner, or a community. If you live alone, I hope you find like-minded or supportive people who would also like to experience the excitement of living a life of meaning.

why write this book?

beginning at home

While thousands of people on many different continents and from all walks of life have taken courses in Holistic Management, the key to continued practice is deep ownership in your holisticgoal (your vision) and your ability to make decisions that are in line with that goal. So while it is certainly possible to practice Holistic Management in a corporation or bureaucracy, the smaller the unit, the more effective we can be in creating the life we want.

For that reason, one of the best places to begin making changes or creating a better world is at home. Home is the place where we have the greatest possibility to effect change. In the lingo of Holistic Management, it is the most manageable whole. Home has often been idealized as a sanctuary from the daily trials and tribulations of the outside world. Some homes do offer that, while others can be a living hell. But homes also have the potential to carry us on our journey, not just hold us safe in the harbor or locked in the brig. In his poem, "On Houses," Kahlil Gibran speaks of that third possibility: home as a sail, not an anchor.

In other words, our homes can provide us a place to feel safe and help us create the world we want. With Holistic Management, we can count on the rest of our "crew" to help clarify the values about which we feel strongly. As a team we can live our collective lives built on those values. Likewise, we can understand where and how we could support each other, recognize each person's responsibility in what we create, hold each other accountable, acknowledge both "successes" and insights, and experience the pleasure of helping each other get what we want out of life. That experience can be scary or exciting or both.

I can't say I've experienced success or made wise decisions every time since I started practicing Holistic Management in my daily life. However, I can certainly say that the number of times I experience that deep sense of creation, see the bigger picture, and achieve the results I want have dramatically increased. I have also heard many different people's stories (people with little similarity except their desire for a better life — whatever that meant to them) who all report the same evolution and change in their lives. So I wanted to write this book and share the experiences of ordinary individuals doing extraordinary things.

choosing a metaphor

As I began thinking about how to explain the process of practicing Holistic Management, I searched for a metaphor that would graphically represent life's journey and how Holistic Management can help on that journey. So I chose the metaphor of a sailing ship as the essence of life's journey, particularly within the context of family or community. Like a ship, we are affected by many elements and events that are beyond our control, but not wholly unpredictable. A seasoned sailor skillfully ascertains the signs of storms and calms, knows where there are shoals, and understands his/her responsibility. Furthermore, such a sailor remains calm in the face of adversity, navigates, and possesses any other number of skills that will make the difference between a safe and productive voyage and disaster.

In other words, we can't control many things in life, but we can influence many results if we are willing to make the effort because we know how important the results are to us. This philosophy doesn't imply that everyone who feels stuck or unlucky deserves what he gets. Nor does it suggest that if an individual had enough moral character she wouldn't have all her problems. Rather, this philosophy or worldview offers hope. If we all take the time to really know what is important to us, what makes us tick, and how we can access all of our multiple talents, then we can truly make a contribution to our own life and the lives of others.

how to use this book

To make the most of this book, integrate Holistic Management with anything you do. The great thing about Holistic Management is that it is a collaborative process. That means that you can use it with any other process you have found that helps you create the life you want. So if at any point you want or need an outside perspective, seek support from a friend or a professional (therapist, minister, Holistic Management® Certified Educator, coach, etc.) and integrate their perspective with what you are learning.

The exercises sprinkled throughout this book and in Appendix 1 will help you practice the skills and concepts covered in the following pages. Most of these exercises can be done in a day, although some take more time. If you find you don't like an exercise, determine what the intent of it is and then adapt it to your mode of learning. For example, if an exercise asks you to discuss something, but one or more members of your group is having difficulty with the discussion, then turn the exercise into a physical, artistic, or musical activity. Instead of discussing an idea, draw it, role-play a situation involving that idea, or make up a song about it. Keep adapting the exercises to your specific needs. You can always do the same exercise in different ways to meet everyone's needs. The exercises shouldn't feel like work as they were designed to be playful and exploratory. Keep that attitude as you do them or adapt them.

To deepen the learning from any exercise, ask Adaptive Learning questions after completing the exercise. Examples of adaptive learning questions are: 1) What happened? 2) What did we learn? 3) How do we feel? It's usually helpful to ask these three questions in that order because people often need to summarize an event before they can synthesize or analyze it.

It is myth, not a mandate, a fable, not a logic, and symbol rather than a reason by which men are moved.

—Sophocles

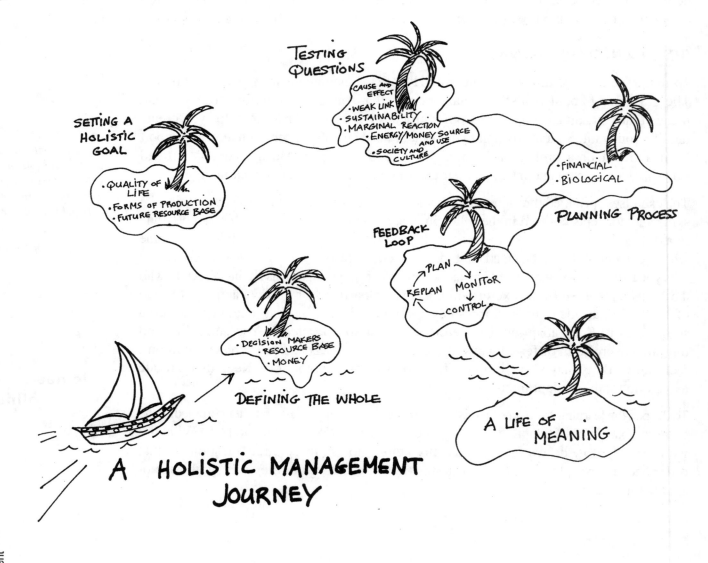

TESTING QUESTIONS
• CAUSE AND EFFECT
• WEAK LINK
• SUSTAINABILITY
• MARGINAL REACTION
• ENERGY/MONEY SOURCE AND USE
• SOCIETY AND CULTURE

SETTING A HOLISTIC GOAL
• QUALITY OF LIFE
• FORMS OF PRODUCTION
• FUTURE RESOURCE BASE

FINANCIAL
• BIOLOGICAL

PLANNING PROCESS

FEEDBACK LOOP
PLAN
REPLAN   MONITOR
CONTROL

DECISION MAKERS
• RESOURCE BASE
• MONEY

DEFINING THE WHOLE

A LIFE OF MEANING

A HOLISTIC MANAGEMENT JOURNEY

acquiring new navigational tools

Holistic Management and holism

what is Holistic Management?

For those of you not familiar with Holistic Management, it involves a new decision-making framework and management process that Allan Savory (co-founder of Holistic Management International) created. For the last 30 years, thousands of people all over the world have continued to develop and evolve this process through their own experiences. Because Holistic Management incorporates a holistic perspective or point of view, it helps people see the bigger picture, analyze it, and make decisions and/or take action in response to that information. However, what is most unique about Holistic Management is that it provides a framework that helps people address all of their immediate and future needs including their social (personal and spiritual values), environmental, and financial needs. In other words, Holistic Management helps you figure out what you really want then makes sure that what you do delivers it.

That's why Holistic Management is important. Through the holisticgoal setting and testing questions (and other aspects of this process you'll learn later), Holistic Management offers people a way to make decisions that will move them toward what they want, not in reaction to what they don't want. As resources become more limited, and the world population becomes more interdependent, any process that helps us to think about the long-term ramifications of our actions is a valuable tool. And the best part of all is that much of this extra effort doesn't feel like work. Many people have found that the more success they have at really knowing what they want and using the Holistic Management framework to help achieve those results, the more they enjoy or feel ready to meet and make use of the challenges and opportunities that life offers.

To understand the different parts of the Holistic Management process or journey, look at the diagram on the facing page. As you can see, the ship you are sailing is you or the whole you are managing. As you learn in the next chapter, you will encounter the ecosystem processes through which nature functions throughout this journey so you need to consider them each time you begin the next step in your journey.

The Holistic Management process starts with defining the whole (understanding what the boundaries are to what you want to manage). Another way of looking

key concepts in this chapter

what is Holistic Management?

holism is like a pair of eyeglasses

"part-thinking" leads to more unintended consequences

a goal pulls. problems push.

when people are motivated, there is little need for discipline

making conscious decisions means retraining human nature

making the most of your resources is fun

at this piece of the process is describing those people within the particular whole you are managing who make decisions (decision makers), the people and natural resources that you impact directly or who affect you and upon which you depend (your resource base) and the money available to you.

Once you have a clear sense of your whole, you're ready to create your holisticgoal. A holisticgoal includes: your *quality of life* statement (describing what you want in your life now for that whole you are managing whether as a family, business, or organization); a *forms of production* statement (what you have to produce to create that quality of life); and a *future resource base* description (what you, your land—whether you own it or not—and your community have to be like far into the future in order to sustain the quality of life you want now).

With a written holisticgoal, you now have a clear sense of direction that includes all that you want to achieve in the whole you have defined. Once you have created your holisticgoal, you need to use it to make sure you are making progress toward it. The testing questions (Chapter 6) are designed to help you make good decisions that will continually move you toward the life you want. You can run any decision, large or small, through these testing questions.

> **THE BLIND MEN AND THE ELEPHANT**
>
> One day five blind men went for a walk. Suddenly they came across an unfamiliar object. The first touched the elephant's trunk and said, "It is like a big snake." In the meantime, the second blind man had come alongside of him and felt the elephant's tusk. "No," he argued, "It is like a sword." The third had come alongside the second and felt the elephant's ear. "You are both wrong," he cried. "It is like a fan." By then the fourth and fifth blind men had moved around the others, the first touching the elephant's leg and the second his tail. The one proclaimed that the elephant was like a tree and the other that it was like a whip, and they all argued long into the night.

Of course, some decisions are more complicated than others in that they require more planning and more steps to accomplish. At least yearly you will need to do some type of planning to make sure that you give sufficient attention to high priority ideas or projects before you move on to items with a lower priority or return.

The last essential area of the Holistic Management process is the feedback loop, which takes into account that all actions have unintended consequences. Because you don't know what those unintended consequences might be, you need to monitor (create monitoring criteria and use them) to make sure you are either staying on track with a plan or catching yourself as soon as possible before going off plan. That way you can either adjust your actions to get back on plan or replan.

holism as eyeglasses

In a nutshell, holism is the idea that the universe consists of wholes that we cannot understand or engage with effectively if viewed in isolation, or as parts. The notion of holism has existed in many cultures (particularly those of indigenous people), and certainly has influenced decisions about land use, interaction with immigrants, and tribal custom. And while many people intellectually accept the concept of holism, actually viewing the world through "holistic eyeglasses" is rather challenging (particularly for those of us from a Western culture that was founded on the concepts of individualism).

Some people use the word *paradigm* to describe the idea of seeing the world through a certain set of eyeglasses. A paradigm is the idea that people have developed or learned a given belief system or worldview through which they see or experience reality. And because our paradigms affect what we believe to be true, they also affect what we choose to hear, see, and believe. In other words, they shape our reality. To view things holistically often requires what is known as a *paradigm shift.*

Before a paradigm shift, you respond from instinct or routine. After a paradigm shift, you question your assumptions and beliefs with a willingness to shift or change those beliefs. Such a shift can be both challenging and exhilarating. Moreover, ask anyone who has experienced such a shift and they will tell you that not only would they not return to the old way, they often can't. Thus, a true paradigm shift can be irreversible. But, not to worry. You can't experience a paradigm shift until you are ready.

To shift a paradigm, you must question the assumptions and beliefs that you hold. A belief is different from a value in that a belief is an opinion that you were probably

---

| **exercise 1-1.**

paradigm shift

purpose:

experience a paradigm shift | Below is just one of many games you can do to help people break through a paradigm. We constantly use our beliefs to create order and meaning from what we observe. Sometimes that can be helpful, but paradigms sometimes hold us back from seeing new information, or interpreting that information in a different way. I recommend a book like *Silver Bullets,* by Karl Rohnke, if your group likes these types of games. This exercise can be a warm-up for "Exploring Beliefs" (a1-1) in Appendix 1.

Use four straight lines to connect all the dots below without lifting your pen or retracing over a line.

   *   *   *

   *   *   *

   *   *   *

The answer is in the back of the book at the beginning of Appendix 1.

If you haven't already seen this puzzle, the reason that most people have difficulty solving it is because they stay within the bounds of the square created by the dots. In this way, paradigms or beliefs often limit us and keep us from seeing the myriad alternatives outside the "box." |

Loyalty to petrified opinion never yet broke a chain or freed a human soul.

—*Mark Twain*

taught or learned that doesn't necessarily transcend cultures (i.e. how to honor the dead). A value is an ideal that tends to be more universal (i.e. desire for family, health, etc.) By questioning your beliefs, you find out what other beliefs are behind them and where those beliefs limit you.

In the case of holism (specifically Holistic Management), the usual symptoms of a paradigm shift are:

- You understand that because you are part of a whole that in turn affects many other wholes, you really are important (as are the other wholes because of their impact on you).

- Because you are important, you are accountable. And because you are accountable, your decisions must have integrity.

- You begin to notice the pattern and structure of how things function. Consequently, you have a greater trust in your ability to work with these processes and thrive.

- You take more time to make major decisions (or at least ask deeper questions to get more information before you make a decision).

- The world has a greater sense of order and meaning because you are able to see the big picture better than before.

- You have a deeper sense of how to contribute, and you have a greater sense of well being.

In time of drastic change it is the learners who inherit the future.

—Eric Hoffer

The saying goes that hindsight is 20/20. But what if we could improve our foresight by using certain tools or concepts to make the most of our resources? Just as someone who is genetically nearsighted can have 20/20 vision with eyeglasses, we can learn to make better decisions because we have the framework (holistic eyeglasses) that helps us see the big picture and begin to understand what some of the long-term consequences of our decisions will be.

Obviously we can't predict the future or control nature, but we can understand how natural processes function so that we know the right questions to ask. If we have that framework, then we are better able to grow as individuals and families.

Some people think holism is just about interconnected parts. Of course, the perception of "parts" means that you think things have a boundary or border that distinguish them from something else. To help understand the concept of holism better, remember that the concept of holism includes the chemistry or relationships that make a whole more than the sum of its parts. Some people call this chemistry "synergy."

A cake is one example of synergy. Lay out all the ingredients for making a cake from scratch (a box cake already has many of the ingredients combined), and have your children taste each item or talk about what each item does. You can even experiment with small batches. Children quickly understand that cake is quite different from the eggs, oil, flour, sugar, etc. Those items are a cake's ingredients but are not a cake until

exercise 1-2.

the holistic viewpoint

purpose:

to better understand how the world functions as wholes within wholes.

Look at the following picture. Try to see everything that is connected or influenced by that object and how it relates to you.

Take this apple as an example. In this apple I see sunshine, a cloud and a honeybee. For without sun, rain and the bee there would not be an apple. There must be fertile living soil, a healthy tree, and a person to care for it. There may be fertilizers and pesticides. To harvest the apple, there must be a picker and someone to package it (or process it at home), a place to store it, and a truck to transport it to the store where it is sold. Eventually the apple becomes waste in the form of sewage and organic matter in a landfill or someone's compost pile. Many tools and resources are used to create, use and dispose of this apple: sunshine, technology, living organisms, fossil fuels, human creativity, money, and labor.

Now it's your turn:

1) Have the family choose one of these pictures—or a picture that you enjoy, e.g., of children playing, a city, a forest, a car.

2) Try to see everything that connects or relates to the object

3) Use all of your senses in the process.

For an additional holism exercise, see "Holism Exercise" (a1-2) in Appendix 1.

Created by Holistic Management® Certified Educator Cindy Dvergsten.

Taking a new step, uttering a new word is what people fear most.

—Fyodor Dostoyevski

you put them together in a certain way. In their synergy, they become more than they could be alone. Likewise, a family is different from each individual parent, relative, child and extended family member. Those "ingredients" have the potential to blend. The potential chemistry and relationships between those individuals can produce something greater than any of those individuals could alone. How a family understands and uses that principle can greatly affect the family as a whole. For an additional exercise on synergy, see "Synergy Exercise" (a1-3) in Appendix 1.

a goal pulls. problems push.

One of the key concepts of Holistic Management is that the holisticgoal (vision) pulls you toward what you want, rather than helping you resist (fight against) what you don't want. In other words, people spend time identifying positive outcomes that become reasons for making a decision to create what they want, rather than focusing on negative consequences (problems or crises) to motivate them.

If you look at the way people make decisions, it is more often than not based on problem-solving rather than decision-making: "Johnny watches too much TV" rather than "What do I want for Johnny and how can I help create that environment." "We don't have enough money" rather than "How do I want to create profit." "You eat too much" rather than "How can we create healthy eating habits." With that problem-solving paradigm, our goal is for other people to change their behavior, and I haven't had much luck in making that happen. I have had success at determining what my desired outcome is then making decisions to move toward it. The results have been rather surprising at times.

Children, and many adults, often make decisions based on short-term consequences (like immediate gratification) or on what will bring the least negative consequence. For example, when I talked with my son, Ben (age nine), about how he made decisions, he implied that he usually based his decisions on issues of health (not wanting to get

Did you ever observe to whom the accidents happen? Chance favors only the prepared mind.

—Louis Pasteur

SOCCER CAMP

The other day, Ben came home from his first day at soccer camp. He had really looked forward to this camp because he had had a good time there the year before. This year, however, he didn't have his best friend there with him. In fact, he didn't know anyone. Unfortunately, there were kids in his group who harassed each other if anyone made a mistake. Ben came home very disheartened by the experience. Because I immediately became engaged in the conflict, I asked him what he thought the ideal response to their comments would be. Without a moment's hesitation, his eyes lit up and he said "Yell back at them and punch them in the nose!"

I then asked him if that response was in line with how he wanted to be perceived and how he described himself (healthy, happy, creative, caring, kind, and thoughtful). He knew it wasn't, but he still felt angry and preferred to remain righteously indignant. We then went on to a series of specific responses he could try to stop the kids' harassment. The discussion I was leading was not about things he could do to create the soccer camp he wanted because I had fallen into the problem-solving mode of responding to a conflict.

As soon as he stated that he wanted a soccer camp where everyone had fun and treated each other with respect, I then remembered to ask the question, "Was anyone acting that way today?" In the previous discussion he said that the kids had been mean 90% of the time. Suddenly, when I started reframing the questions with the perspective of what he wanted (i.e., "So how do you want the kids to act at soccer camp?"), the percentage dropped to 80% because he remembered the other events of the day. He was also smiling more instead of explaining why he couldn't do anything to change the situation.

Ironically, as soon as he started remembering the good stuff, he also readjusted his vision of what would be an "acceptable ratio" of good to bad times. In the previous conversation he had settled for 25/75, now he wanted 40/60 (a far more appropriate expectation in my mind).

So I made a deal with him. I'd pay him five dollars to perform a grand experiment. He had to keep in his mind that he wanted everyone there to be friendly and have fun. He then had to act accordingly. If in the past he had responded to their unkind words with some of his own, he now had to focus on what he would say if they were his friends. For example, when they said, "Can't you do any better than that," he would reply in the affirmative ("Yes, I think I can.") instead of what he had initially tried — "Let's see you do any better." If they made a goal, he'd say, "Good shot." These were his ideas. He agreed to remember to do this in at least half of his interactions and to tell me the ratio of good to bad times as the outcome.

The next day he came home from camp with the news that the ratio was 99/1. We were all taken aback at how well it had worked, and he had had the experience of creating what he wanted (a success that will remind him of what he can accomplish), even if he had initially been motivated externally by money. I have certainly given him money to do chores (to teach him to contribute to the family and learn how to clean), so the idea of motivating him to try a new method of decision-making seemed even more important.

But what struck me so profoundly from that experience, was how easily I fell into a problem-solving mode or at least responded from that mode in my suggestions and questions. When I had remembered to ask him what he wanted, it was like a veil had lifted for both of us.

hurt) or social need (not wanting to make his friends mad). In other words, he thought a good decision was one in which you avoided negative consequences. He didn't believe he had enough power to create what he wanted, rather, he was busy making sure things didn't happen to him. I think there are a lot of adults that view the world that way as well. It seems a lot easier to rail at God or the world than to consider what we might be doing to interfere with what we want.

"parts-thinking" leads to more unintended consequences

Many other processes explore the importance of values clarification and the need for a goal to move you toward a desired outcome. But Holistic Management has a specific goal setting structure to help you create a holisticgoal. If people divide their lives and goals into various categories with no framework to see how one goal or objective might affect another, then their pursuit of one goal can be to the detriment of another.

In Holistic Management, we always attempt to look at the world holistically. Therefore, a holisticgoal incorporates the core values of the people who created it (We want quality time together and recreation), rather than specific outcomes (We'll buy a new boat this year). Those kinds of specific plans come later, after you form your

exercise 1-3.

contributing factor exercise

purpose:

move people from problem-solving to decision-making

This exercise is designed to help make people conscious of how they contribute to a situation. They can then define what they want, and use the opportunity to change a situation in which they have felt powerless.

1) Pick one family member to talk about a situation that has been bothering her.

2) Let her explain and complain for five minutes. Ask questions if you are unclear what she is unhappy about and why. Repeat back to her what you thought she said, then find out what she would like to have happen in that situation (how she would like that situation to be).

3) Get her to stay in the positive (i.e., "People cooperate and are friendly" instead of "People won't be mean").

4) Have her list the way she would have to behave to make that outcome happen (such as modeling the behavior she wants). Be specific.

5) Have her make a verbal contract with the rest of the family to try behaving that way for one day (whether at school or work or around the house).

6) Have her keep track of the number of interactions in which she remembered to behave the way she agreed to.

7) Create a scale of "success" and have her rate her current placement on that scale as well as where she would like to be. For example, if her interaction with someone is currently a 5 on a scale of 1 to 10, she might decide that she wants to advance to a 7 by behaving differently.

8) Report back to the family at the next meeting or at dinner.

<u>Contributing Factor Exercise</u>

Problem:
Top Three Reasons   1.
         2.
         3.
How you want situation to be:
Desired Behaviors:
What beliefs do you need to have or what behaviors do you need to do?
1.
2.
3.
         a.
         b.
         c.

Scale of success
Now
1   3   5   7   10

Where you want to be
1   3   5   7   10

> ## WHAT IS YOUR INTENT?
>
> The sun and the wind were arguing about who was more powerful. So they decided to see if they could make a man take his coat off. The wind blew furiously, trying to blow the coat off, but it only made the man wrap himself more tightly in the coat. The sun came out and made the man so warm that he immediately took off his coat with no struggle because he wanted to.
>
> In this story, the wind saw the man wearing a coat as a problem and proceeded to create a struggle by trying to force it off of him. The sun, on the other hand, thought of the desired outcome (removal of the coat) and what would make the man want to take his coat off. His intent, unlike the wind's, was the desired outcome, not a show of power.
>
> Holistic Management helps us determine what comes easily to us, what we value so deeply that we are moved by it almost effortlessly upon the path of life. Rather than struggling against the winds and calms and reacting to the continual stream of problems that arise, we can move toward our desired outcome. We can choose to create an environment where there is struggle, or one that invites the behavior we would like.

holisticgoal, so that people can test the soundness of a decision in the context of what they really want. In other words, the holisticgoal encompasses what is important to you so you will not forget it when you make a specific plan.

An organizational development principle states that for every intended consequence of an action, there is at least one unintended consequence. But when you take the time to create a framework for how you want to live your life, and practice your ability to see things in wholes (and, therefore, how things relate), then you will find that the number of unintended consequences drops significantly.

Later, after you form your holisticgoal, you will also be able to plan, and monitor those plans, more thoughtfully so you reduce the unintended consequences even more. See Chapter 7 on planning and monitoring.

when people are motivated, there is little need for discipline.

There have been lots of studies about motivation, but the one recurring fact is that people can't motivate others; they can only create an atmosphere in which others can tap their intrinsic motivation and unique gifts from within themselves. In other words, I can't motivate my son to do a particular task in a particular way, but I can help create an environment that allows him to express his talents and contribute to the family.

Holistic Management integrates this concept within its process by emphasizing the importance of all decision makers in a whole contributing to the creation of the holisticgoal and to, therefore, have ownership in it. If one member of the family tries to create the family's holisticgoal alone, it doesn't matter if she has encapsulated the family's values or not, because the rest of the family wasn't included in the process and won't have ownership in the final project. But if the family does have ownership in their holisticgoal, then they will be motivated to move toward their vision.

For an exercise in identifying what motivates you, see "Identifying Motivators" (a1-4) in Appendix 1.

making conscious decisions means retraining human nature

The principles of Holistic Management seem common sense to many people, and they can be (although the definition of common sense can vary from culture to culture). The problem is that most of the time we don't use that common sense when we are in crisis, or we react from an unhelpful learned behavior or instinct. What we've learned or how we are genetically programmed to respond doesn't always serve us well, so adding new tools to our toolbox is an ongoing process of evolution. There are many tools and processes out there. You have only to go to your local bookstore to see the choices for self-improvement techniques. But if you haven't discovered what motivates you and what your unique talents are, then you are less likely to choose (or know how to choose) the resources available to you in the process of retraining your instincts.

With Holistic Management you test each of your decisions toward your holisticgoal. That means that you always have the big picture up in front of each decision (people customize this process to fit their needs and it will be covered in more detail in Chapter 5). Moreover, you have a specific set of questions to ask yourself when testing decisions. These questions help you to look at the situation through those holistic eye-glasses. They also force you to slow down so you aren't making a reactive or instinctive, short-term decision. Putting in that effort before implementing a decision relieves you of most ensuing anxieties about whether that was the best decision you could make, especially if you have already identified early warning monitoring indicators (covered in Chapter Seven).

making the most of your resources is fun

Change can be either a struggle or an enjoyable puzzle. So much depends upon one's attitude. While many people understand this principle, many others advocate change

---

PULLING TOGETHER

Think about the way geese fly. Geese don't migrate alone because they can't go the distance alone. Because each goose can ride on the updraft of the next, sharing the point position in their rotation, they can get 71% more flight distance. If one goose is injured or sick, at least two other geese drop out and stay with the disabled one until it is dead or recovered. That's an instinct that has enabled geese to survive (Adapted from Dr. Roger Fritz' "The Goose Story" in the *ARC News* Vol. 7, No 1, January 1992).

But what instincts do we have that help us evolve, to thrive? Isn't our journey in this life about "thrival," not just survival? Many genetic psychologists believe that our genetic programming (instinct) causes us to respond or make decisions with only the short-term or small picture in mind. It makes sense that if you see a car in your path, your first reaction is to jump away. The problem is that most of the decisions we make today aren't decisions that are helped by this fight-or-flight reaction.

Most of our decisions now require some sense of long-term consequences and the bigger picture because of diminishing resources, increased contact with various cultures (due to a more populated planet and technological advances), and, ironically, our sense that we can do better than what we are doing now. In the past we channeled our want for more into an acquisition of land and resources. We are now faced with the exciting task of focusing our genetic need for more on how to use our human creativity to its fullest with the resources that remain.

out of a doom-and-gloom, fire-and-brimstone approach: "If we don't change the way we behave, our civilization will fail as all others have." While such a prophecy has merit, it shifts us into a problem-solving mode. Consequently, people engage in all sorts of arguments as to how long we have left, which isn't a particularly helpful focus for creating what we want.

Prior to practicing Holistic Management, I muddled along well enough in my life. I made most of my decisions with integrity, tried to keep a bigger picture in mind, planned thoughtfully, and so on. However, Holistic Management attracted me because it provided a framework in which I could co-create a life of meaning. I do not presume to think that I can "create my own reality," or control the future. I can, however, be observant and mindful so that I have a sense of how the universe operates, what I can contribute, and what I truly want. And the sense of joy, excitement, and enthusiasm I have experienced with that focus not only results in a less stressful life, it's actually fun.

conclusion

When you practice Holistic Management, you incorporate a holistic worldview that can open your eyes to many previously unnoticed connections. While such changes require some effort and often go against instinct or training, our greatest ally in this process is our knowledge of what we want. When we have clarity about our desired outcomes we move beyond problem-solving to achieving what we want. And as we better understand how the world operates and our place in it, we are better able to create our desired outcomes and have fun in the process.

Understanding relies on learning the ecosystem processes

I've found that understanding the ecosystem processes helped me really understand how nature works. In turn, I'm better able to make decisions about things like who I buy my food from, why I won't support the local water planning committee's idea on cloudseeding, or what I want to do with my land and garden. Once I could see how the ecosystem processes work, I had a framework from which to ask questions and get more information.

Bonnie Smith

Mother and Program Manager for
Deaf and Hard of Hearing Services
Albuquerque, New Mexico

2

the tides upon which we sail

understanding the ecosystem that sustains us

In the metaphor of the sailing ship, a captain and crew need to know how to read the sea, the weather, the stars, and all the natural clues to make the best decisions possible to get where they are going. Before industrialization, every person in a society had to read natural clues as well, because so much directly depended upon a person's ability to hunt, farm, gather plants, etc. Today much still depends upon everyone's ability to understand his or her environment. While we often don't see that direct connection because of technology and industrialization, that connection still exists.

understanding nature

A basic understanding of how an ecosystem functions enables you to ask a few essential questions that will point you in the right direction when making decisions that affect our environment. So whether you live in the country or the city, in Atlanta or Alberta, understanding the four basic processes that drive the greater ecosystem that sustains us is important. These processes include:

the water cycle: The movement of water and how that movement affects plant and animal (including human) life.

the mineral cycle: The movement of minerals or nutrients and how that movement affects plant, animal, and human life.

energy flow: The movement of energy from the sun through all living (or once living) beings.

community dynamics: The interactions and interrelationships that exist among species that function as wholes or communities.

The first step to understanding how nature works is to recognize that everything in nature is only capable of functioning in what we call wholes. In nature (unlike human thinking) there are no parts and there are no boundaries. For example, think of yourself standing in your garden or your local park. Now, let your mind travel across the land to the seas and across the seas to another continent and into someone else's garden. Didn't your garden blend into your neighbors', into the area around your city or village, into other land or water that eventually connected you to the garden you saw half way around the world? One habitat faded into another without crossing a sharp or defined boundary.

key concepts in this chapter

understanding nature

water cycle

mineral cycle

energy flow

community dynamics

soil cover and the brittleness scale

the importance of these concepts to your community

Likewise, there really are no boundaries between you and the ecosystem that surrounds and sustains all of us. For example, you would not be able to read these words without the energy you obtained in the meals you have eaten over the last few days. For you even to think requires energy from green plants that in turn converted it from raw sunlight to food for all animal life. You wouldn't even be able to breathe the oxygen you need right now without the communities of plants, animals, insects, oceans, grasslands, forests and soils that keep the supply constant. In other words, our ecosystem is just as important to your survival and potential to thrive as your family or business or whatever else you give great importance to.

So where do you begin in this stage of the journey? With the ecosystem processes. To understand the ecosystem processes in a nutshell, look at the diagram on this page. The box in the diagram is a room within which your house, your city, or even the world sits. Through a window on one side of the room you view how the water cycle functions. Through a window on another side you see how the mineral cycle functions, and so on. In other words, each ecosystem process offers you a window to view and understand how the natural world functions around you so you can make better choices as a consumer, citizen, employee, or family member. Likewise, with that knowledge you will have a better understanding of how to set a holisticgoal, test your decisions, and plan.

Speak to the earth, and it shall teach thee.

—Job 12:8

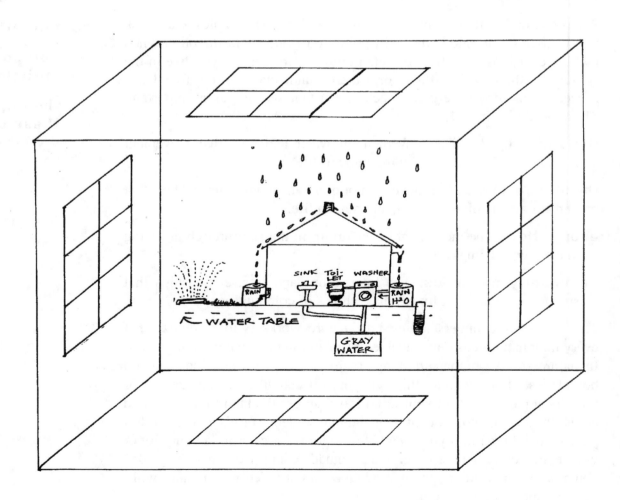

water cycle

The water cycle is probably the easiest of the ecosystem processes to understand because it is a very visible cycle. Once you know what to look for, you can see when it is healthy or not healthy. Most people think of the water cycle in terms of rainfall. Depending on where you live, you could see a lot of it or a little. Water can seem like a precious resource or something you tolerate. But, fresh water is a minute proportion of the earth's water and through rising populations and world-wide environmental degradation it is becoming a scarce commodity. You, like many, may already pay more for clean drinking water per gallon or liter than you do for the gas that runs your car. And most scientists and politicians agree that in the coming millennium fresh water will be the scarcest major resource worldwide, with all the potential to lead to enormous conflict.

On all land, fresh water falls from the sky mainly as rain or snow. Once it hits the earth, most of it should ideally soak into the soil. From there it should ideally pass out through growing plants back to the atmosphere or remain in the soil until enough accumulates to feed permanent and perennial rivers, and to sustain sponges, springs, wetlands, and underground aquifers. The condition of the soil surface is key to the effectiveness of the water cycle: is it covered or is it largely bare and exposed? You also need to consider the amount of organic matter in the soil that gives it most of its porosity and sponge-like ability to hold water.

If much of the soil surface between plants is bare and exposed, two main things go wrong with the water cycle and both can have devastating effects on your life no matter where you live or what your business. First, whenever the rate of rainfall or snowmelt is rapid, the water is not able to penetrate the soil surface quickly enough and much of the water flows off to cause floods. Secondly, if the land is flat and the soil exposed then when the rainfall is light or the snowmelt is gradual most of the water that does soak in does not reach plant roots or even remain underground. Like your hairdryer, the wind and sun dry the uppermost soil. Moreover, like blotting paper, it draws water from the soil below. In turn, most of the water evaporates back to the atmosphere without feeding plants, rivers, springs, sponges, wetlands or underground aquifers.

The result is increasing frequency and severity of droughts, and drying up of the land and its rivers, aquifers and springs. This is called desertification and is now spreading world-wide at more than 400,000 acres a day and resulting in millions of environmental refugees, human suffering, poverty, conflict, genocide and even war. The ever increasing Mississippi, California or Texas floods and mudslides, with their enormous costs are evidence of how poorly the water cycle is functioning even in a country with vast financial and scientific resources. With experts blaming these floods on such things as high rainfall, or the levees built to contain seasonally-high flows, the average citizen is left unaware of what the underlying causes are and how he or she can take proactive action.

So, in a healthy or effective water cycle, plants can use the precipitation where it falls. Moreover, because the water stays relatively close to where it lands, it doesn't carry valuable topsoil away or flood low-lying areas.

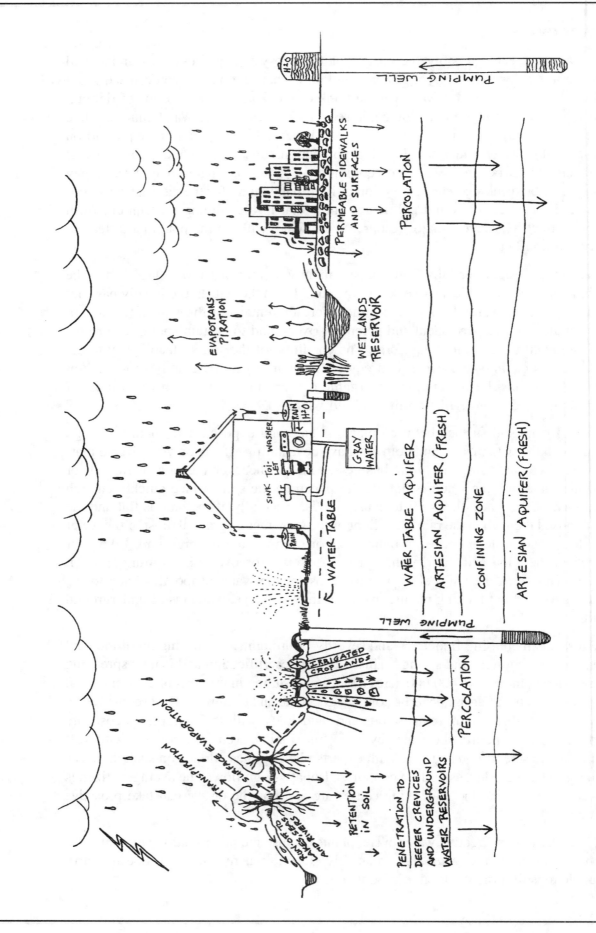

The water cycle

What can you look for to determine the health of the water cycle? The condition of the land or the ground is a good clue. If the ground is bare, then the water will either evaporate or run off rapidly. If the ground is covered with plants and mulch or litter that can help to absorb the water like sponges, then the land can drink in the water and store it for plant use later as the ground dries out.

Below is a series of questions to determine the health of the water cycle in your community:

- Where does the water go after you use it?

- Where does your water come from?

- How much ground is bare or covered with a hard surface such as roofs, streets, sidewalks, parking lots, etc.?

- What could you do to help cover the ground with living plants or plant litter?

- What would need to change to make the water cycle more effective?

- What would you need to do to help water cycle closer to you so the living beings near you (including you) could use it?

- Who could you work with in your area to help create a healthier water cycle for your community? Who can provide you with additional information about the water cycle in your area (municipal water utility employees, conservation agencies, etc.)?

| **exercise 2-1.**

 a water drop's journey

 purpose:

 understanding the water cycle | 1) Pretend you are a drop of water.

 • How far do you have to travel and how long does it take to get from when you first fell to the ground from the sky to a kitchen sink?

 • How long before you return to the atmosphere?

 • Who/what do you meet along the way?

 • How do they help or hinder your journey?

 • How do you help them?

 • What could the people in your area do to help?

 • How could you return to the sky through plants or move underground to underground reservoirs?

 • How could you prevent yourself from joining other drops of water and causing floods?

 • How could you prevent yourself from evaporating uselessly back into the sky?

 2) Draw a picture or write a story about your journey. |

If a family living in the city decided that the water cycle within the city was ineffective because the water run-off from the streets and buildings flooded the sewers and polluted the river, they have a number of options. They can work with their neighbors and their municipal government to create separate avenues for sewage and water run-off so that the one doesn't contaminate the other. Or they can decide to install a cistern to capture and use the rainfall from their roof. Or they can decide that because their water comes with great environmental cost that they will take water conservation efforts in their homes by using low-flush or composting toilets, low-flow water fixtures and appliances or, in drier areas, planting plants native to their area that don't require additional water.

mineral or nutrient cycle

Think of the mineral cycle as the circulatory system of the natural world. In your body, blood circulates to bring nutrients to various parts of your body. If you were to sell your blood more rapidly than your body could replenish it, you would either become sick or you would die, depending on the rate you were selling it. While we might help to extend the time before we will have to deal with the consequences of that decision by receiving plasma transfusions, we ultimately need blood in our system, not plasma. The same is true for our soil. If we keep using up the nutrients or minerals in our soil without feeding it or giving it time to regenerate, then we create unhealthy soils with a host of problems. We also have to be careful not to overfeed the soil. Too much fertilizer in your garden, for instance, can kill soil life, make some nutrients in the soil unavailable to plant life, and eventually pollute streams, lakes, and rivers.

In nature, minerals on the land are on the move constantly, being used and reused repeatedly. The nutrients in your body at one time or another over the last few million years were part of uncountable plants, birds, insects, reptiles and dinosaurs. There is no waste. What is waste to one organism is food for another and so on endlessly. Simply expressed, minerals are made available to plants through the actions of trillions of small organisms housed in the organic matter in soil. There can be a billion or more organisms in a tablespoon full of living soil. Plants take many of the minerals above ground into their leaves, stems, flowers or seeds where they feed animals, including humans, or fall eventually to the soil surface. The minerals used by animals also eventually end on the soil surface where, through the action of billions of insects and microorganisms, they break down until they are small enough to pass into the soil carried by water or by animal life in some form.

So the key to an effective mineral cycle is that either living plants, or the dead plant material that forms litter, need to cover the soil. Litter tends to hold moisture and regulate temperatures so that many microorganisms can carry out the breakdown process. This same soil cover, through creating a more effective water cycle, carries minerals underground instead of having them wash away in runoff and floods. And, of course, an effective mineral cycle includes abundant organic material in the soil, which enhances the mass of minute life that not only prevents the minerals from washing out of the soil, but keeps them active and available for reuse.

Every natural resource plays a part in the mineral cycle, whether it is something we eat, wear, use, burn, or put in our compost pile or down the toilet or sink. However, many of the things we consume do not break down quickly, and thus inhibit or slow down the mineral cycle. Likewise, anything mined from underground (petroleum, uranium, aluminum, silver, copper, etc.) is a mineral that took many years to form. Therefore, one way we can help make the mineral cycle in our area more effective is through the decisions we make about what we consume, bearing in mind where and how a product was produced, and how/if it will or can be recycled.

Look at the diagrams of mineral cycles on the next pages. In the effective mineral cycle diagram, you can see some of the choices a person can make to help create a more effective mineral cycle in her community. For example, if we buy produce that was grown locally, we aren't expending additional unnecessary minerals (petroleum) to transport or refrigerate food. Likewise, we can buy produce from a farmer who uses agricultural practices that feed and regenerate the soil with local nutrients (compost, "green manure" plants, livestock, etc.), rather than fertilizers trucked in from distant chemical plants (factories), to increase the effectiveness of the mineral cycle in our community. Moreover, if we recycle our lawn and kitchen waste in a compost pile, those nutrients can feed the soil in our gardens rather than being trucked to a landfill where they can't decompose effectively to feed the soil there.

One of the indicators of an unhealthy cycle is when the minerals no longer cycle because we have set up a structure or system that actually stops them from cycling effectively. A conventional feedlot, where cattle are fattened for slaughter is one example (as is any animal factory). Here, large number of cattle confined to pens eat grain, drink water, consume growth-promoting hormones and antibiotics, and expel bodily waste. Because there are so many animals concentrated in a very small area, there is a lot of waste. That waste either becomes a dangerous substance because it isn't given the proper environment to break down and become a positive resource, or a manure manufacturer trucks it to a farm or further processes it into a soil amendment. In fact, we keep much animal waste, including our own, from cycling in a healthy and effective way because of the way we have structured our environment.

If you look at the diagram of an ineffective mineral cycle, you can see how many of the systems used to obtain food or dispose of waste create an ineffective mineral cycle. If we have to truck our waste, we are giving a valuable resource away. If we put food down a garbage disposal, we are lengthening the amount of time it takes for those minerals to recycle, which means we are contributing to an ineffective mineral cycle. Likewise, what you buy can be made of substances that take longer to break down (a lot of plastic packaging) and thus contribute to an ineffective mineral cycle. Instead you can buy in bulk (less packaging) or from manufacturers who use environmentally-sound substances in both their products and their packaging that can be recycled.

While working to keep soil covered would be the best way of helping to create a healthy mineral cycle, most of us own very little land. But, through our consumer decisions, we contribute to how and where crops are grown, livestock are raised, and cities and suburbs are planned and built. Thus, we have many avenues for affecting the mineral cycle. If we buy food that was grown locally, and under regenerative agricultural practices, rather than food that was trucked in from a mega-farm where 50% of the ground was bare between the plants because of cultivation practices, we can make a difference. Just as citizens during World War II made a difference in the war effort by their individual actions, such as victory gardens and recycling, consumers today can help ensure the health of their environment with similar practices.

An effective mineral cycle.

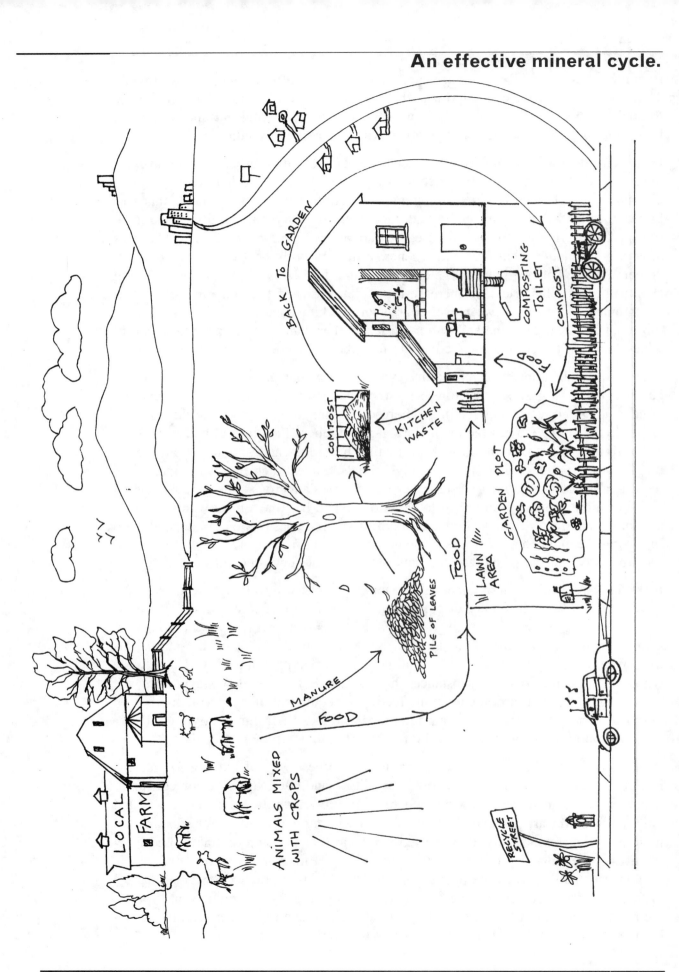

An ineffective mineral cycle.

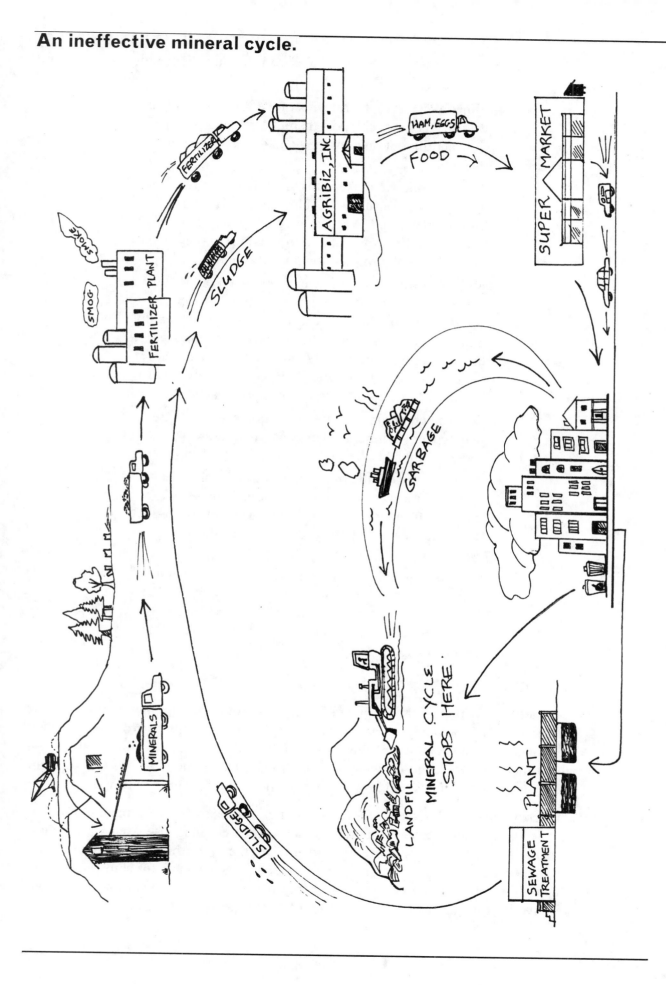

Below is a series of questions that are helpful in judging the health of the mineral cycle:

- What happens to the remains of the food or products we use? (Do we compost them, burn them, put them in a landfill, put them in the garbage disposal, reuse them, etc.?)

- How easy do we make it for the minerals in the food and fiber we consume to cycle? (Where do those nutrients end up? Do they have oxygen and microorganisms to help cycle the minerals?) Are they made of materials that break down easily?

- What environment could we create that would allow nutrients to cycle effectively and locally? (Where could we get products that would help create a healthy mineral cycle? How could we dispose of them once they've outlived their use? How could we dispose of the parts we don't consume?) What kind of products could we buy whose components cycle easily?

- How much ground is bare? How could we increase plant cover (living plants or dead plant litter that serves as mulch, like straw or bark)?

- How do we stop the minerals from cycling? (What systems or structures are we supporting that keep minerals from cycling, e.g., megafarms, megastores, municipal sewage, garbage disposals, feedlots?)

- What feeds life (plants, soil, animals, humans) in my area? (Chemicals, technology, fertilizers, regenerative agriculture, etc.?) Is the input local or is it trucked in? Such shipping makes the mineral cycle wider and more ineffective. (See mineral cycle diagrams on the previous page.)

energy flow

The energy flow is literally the flow of energy from the sun through green, growing plants to all life, including humans. Plants use the sun's energy to grow. We then eat the plants or eat an animal that eats those plants so that we can consume that energy, which fuels our bodies to do what we need to do. This is how we use the sunlight energy trapped by plants and how we benefit from sunlight energy flow.

Our ecosystem runs on solar energy. Everything in it depends on the plant's ability to capture sunlight and convert it to a form that feeds everything else—bugs, microbes, animals, and humans. The more plants we have, the more the available energy. So the greater the energy flow, the more food or energy is available for something to eat which ultimately means more food or energy for us. You can make that flow more effective if you can increase the amount of green, growing leaves that capture that

exercise 2-2.	Take the following mineral cycle inventory to see how effective the mineral cycle is in your home. Answer the questions by circling the appropriate response and total your score using the numbers at the top of the column you select for each answer.					
mineral cycle inventory						
		_1_	_2_	_3_	_4_	_5_
purpose: find out how effective the mineral cycle is in your home	1) What percentage of your kitchen waste do you compost rather than throw into a disposal or garbage bag?	100%	75%	50%	25%	0%
	2) What percentage of your yard waste do you compost rather than burn or put in the trash?	100%	75%	50%	25%	0%
	3) What percentage of your bodily waste do you compost rather than flush?	100%	75%	50%	25%	0%
	4) What percentage of your yard is covered with plants or mulch?	100%	75%	50%	25%	0%
	5) What percentage of your food comes from local sources or do you grow yourself?	100%	75%	50%	25%	0%
	6) What percentage of your food is regeneratively produced (producers attempt to address the environmental impact of production and regenerate soil)?	100%	75%	50%	25%	0%
	7) How many pounds of garbage do you produce per person per week?	1#	3#	5#	7#	10#+
	8) Do you recycle or reuse resources? Always (1) Sometimes (3) Never (5) Often (2) Infrequently (4)					
	9) What percentage of your purchased household non-food items do you make or do you know are manufactured with sustainable/regenerative practices (i.e. toilet paper, paper towels, dish detergent, laundry soap, etc.)?	100%	75%	50%	25%	0%
	10) What percentage of your clothes do you make or are manufactured with sustainable/regenerative practices? Consider the differences between cotton versus organic cotton, or natural dyes versus synthetics or petrochemical dyes, etc. (These are some hard decisions to make and the choices may be limited. However, we need to look at the environmental cost of our clothing.)	100%	75%	50%	25%	0%

scoring:

Score	Condition of Mineral Cycle
10-15	Robust
16-25	OK
26-35	Questionable
36-45	Hurting
46-50	Dangerously Ineffective

sunshine, and lengthen the time over which plants are actively growing and thus converting energy.

For that reason, if we want to increase energy flow, we need to plan ways that we can capture solar energy through photosynthesis. How we plan our cities, what we do with our private agricultural lands, our public lands, or our lawns and gardens will greatly affect the amount of energy flow. Because the key to maximizing energy flow on the land is how well the soil is covered, followed closely by the diversity of plant and animal life, we should aim to have one hundred percent of the soil surface covered all of the time to maximize the flow of energy to life. But, in many environments that can be difficult to achieve without an additional piece of information, which we'll cover later in this chapter.

Below is a series of questions to determine the extent of the energy flow where you live:

- What percentage of plant-covered ground to bare ground or developed (houses, pavement, etc.) ground is in my neighborhood?
- What could I do to increase the percentage of plant-covered ground?
- What plants grow or convert energy at different times of the year? How can I lengthen the amount of time that plants can grow (e.g. add mulch or increase the variety of cold and warm weather plants).
- How can I personally help to increase the energy flow in my area?

community dynamics

exercise 2-3. **the dart test** **purpose:** **explore the idea of energy flow**	1) Get a dart, a sheet of paper, and a pen. Go into your backyard, to a park, or a farm. 2) Choose a central location and mark it. With your eyes closed, throw the dart (be sure no one is around or that they stand behind you). 3) Note whether the dart landed on some plant or on bare, rocky or sealed (with a hard substance) ground. If you live in a year-round moist environment, you might have very little bare ground in your yard. However, if you look at whether the plants present have narrow or broad leaves and if they are green or not, you have another indicator of the amount of energy they are converting. Broad leaves convert more than narrow leaves; plants that are no longer green cannot convert sunlight energy. When there is a mix of broad and narrow leaves, at least some of the plants will convert energy in the spring, summer, and fall, rather than only at one time of year. 4) Return to your central location and throw again. Do 25 random throws. 5) From your total calculate the percentage of bare ground. (Multiply each total by 4 to get your percentage.) If you have time and interest, throw the dart 100 times for a more accurate figure. 6) Brainstorm 10 ways you could increase plants or decrease bare or sealed ground in whatever areas you threw your darts. What ways can you extend the growing season of the plants you have (mulch to return moisture or warmth, or plant different species that grow at different times of the year). If you could implement your plans, what percentage of ground could you cover with plants or organic matter (i.e. mulch)?

Biological communities may start simply from a fresh pool of water or recently exposed rock or soil surface when pioneering species invade the new site, but they soon become increasingly complex. They remain dynamic throughout their existence in that they are never static but always changing. As a biological community develops complexity in the form of thousands of species (from microorganisms to large trees and animals) it may appear that nothing is happening. However, if you look more closely and in detail, the community is, in fact, continually changing—plants and animals are establishing or being born, aging, dying, decaying. The proportions of the many species also keep changing depending upon weather or other factors.

In almost every biological community, to many people's surprise, there is more life in the soil than on top of it. Thus, a healthy pasture carrying many cattle, for instance, can carry a greater weight per acre of earthworms than cattle. Even more amazing, this scenario ignores all the billions of other organisms per tablespoon, and the massive root structures of the plants that would add even more weight and activity to the subsurface total.

The key to the advance of any biological community to greater complexity is soil cover. If some factor constantly creates or maintains bare ground, the community will lose complexity and begin to break down. Conversely, if bare soil is by some means covered with living plants or dead plant material (litter), the community will begin to build up and complexity increase.

A very important principle of community dynamics is that when any community is simple and developing, or is reduced to the simplicity of a few species, it is more unstable and liable to more violent fluctuations in the numbers within some species. This is commonly seen in outbreaks of some plants, insects, birds or rodents to the point that we call them names such as "weeds," "noxious plants," "pests,"or "problem animals" and go to endless (almost always highly costly and unsuccessful) measures to eradicate them.

When you plant a large expanse of lawn to one species, for example, you are creating a simplified community. "Weeds" and insect "pests" will invade it immediately and you must take measures to eradicate them, usually with herbicides and insecticides, if you want to maintain your simplified community. Alternatively, you could spend time and money to create a healthy landscape that can thrive with little or no input by increasing the complexity of the community rather than trying to simplify it further.

You can tell a healthy community by the number of species, the types of species, the numbers within each species, and the diversity of age within those species. The more diversity the better because increased complexity means increased stability. Therefore, any time you damage one species, or remove it, you are damaging or impacting other species, and the stability of the community. Likewise, if you want to protect one species you need to create a healthy environment that supports the thriving community necessary to sustain not only that species, but also many others. Certain environments encourage certain types of species so you need to determine what environment you want to create, not respond to one species in isolation.

Below is a series of questions to determine the health of the communities in your area:

- What kind of diversity do we have in our backyard or garden (species, numbers within species, or age)?
- How stable is that community? How much fluctuation is there in the populations of various species?
- How do we encourage complexity and stability?
- What do we do to discourage complexity and stability?
- What could we do to encourage more complexity and stability?
- What species thrive in the environment we've created here?
- What species do we want?

| **exercise 2-4.**

a dynamic community

purpose:

identifying species | 1) Pick a local area you would like to visit or about which you want to learn (your yard or a park).

2) Go to the area with paper and pencil and identify and record as many species as possible. You can be as generic or specific as you want (red spiky flower = Indian Paintbrush). You don't need to know names as much as observe all the species present. You might think there aren't very many but keep looking and see if you can discover more. Keep a tally of the numbers of each species. Don't forget to include all plants (trees, bushes, grasses, and flowers) and animals (mammals, birds, reptiles, fish, and insects). Dig up a shovelful of earth and see how many worms and insects you can count.

3) Make a sketch of that area including all the details you recorded. Color it in and make a legend for what symbol represents which species. You can even put the numbers of each species within the legend so you can identify which areas have more species than others.

4) Now go to some other places near that area (lawns, gardens, parks, etc.) to see what other species might exist although they weren't in your tally. Make a list of all those species.

5) What type of habitat does each species prefer—hot, dry, and light or cool, moist, and shade.

6) Now return to your drawing. Which of these new species can you add? Where would they fit best? Try to intermingle the new species with the old ones to create a more complex picture. If your lawn is all one type of grass, sketch in other grasses, some flowers, trees, or bushes. See if you can double the number of species from one picture to the next.

7) How does that picture look now? What steps would you need to take to begin creating the habitat you have identified? If it is public land, such as a park, who would you need to contact to get support for such a project? Think of all the people who might be interested. |

soil cover and the brittleness scale

Now that you understand the importance of soil cover and how it impacts each of the ecosystem processes, it's time to learn about a critical piece of the environmental puzzle that is a more recent discovery. Until recently, environments were classified according to the main form of plant life present—grasslands, savanna-woodlands, forests, and so on. Now there is a more fundamental way of classifying any environment that is based on, among other things, how easy or difficult it is to keep soil covered. Mainly living and dead plants provide soil cover. The bases of living plants cover a certain amount of ground, but quite a lot of the soil surface between the plants can still be bare. Here, dead plants, in the form of litter or mulch, often provide the bulk of the cover.

In what we call *non-brittle environments,* which are moist year-round, it is extremely difficult to create vast areas where the soil between plants is bare. As fast as soil is exposed it covers over with some form of plant. Humans are only able to keep ground cleared with the continuous use of machinery, such as we do in today's large scale crop farming. Ancient cities that collapsed and were abandoned in such environments covered over quickly in vegetation.

In *brittle environments,* where rainfall and humidity are erratic, it becomes very easy to create billions of acres where the soil between plants is bare. This exposure results in the breakdown of all four of the ecosystem processes. The abandoned cities of past civilizations in these environments are generally covered by desert sands.

All the world's environments fall somewhere on a continuous scale between non-brittle and very brittle. However, approximately two-thirds of Earth's land surface is brittle to some degree, and thus prone to soil exposure. Nature did have a way of thwarting this potential problem. Up until fairly recent times, herding-type animals helped ensure that bare ground was kept to a minimum in brittle environments, which is where the herding species and the pack-hunting predators that kept them on the move, evolved. The once prolific herds trampled down dead vegetation (for litter) and broke up sealed soil surfaces so new plants could grow. And just as important, they consumed the mass of dried-up vegetation left at the end of the growing season, so that new growth wouldn't be choked out when the new growing season commenced. In this way, the animals helped keep the minerals cycling and the plants healthy and able to reproduce (and cover soil).

The wild herds are gone, of course, and we are left mainly with livestock that no longer bunch and keep on the move because the pack-hunting predators are also gone. Instead, many agricultural producers use fire to help remove the dead vegetation. In other words, we are left with a very large landmass that isn't functioning properly because a vital component is missing. Fortunately, livestock can now be managed to simulate what occurred when wild herds and their predators were present, and can begin to restore the land to health.

For more information on how we do this, see *Holistic Management: A New Framework for Decision Making* by Allan Savory with Jody Butterfield.

We didn't inherit the land from our fathers. We are borrowing it from our children.

—Amish saying

the importance of these concepts to your community

Increasingly, more and more of us are seeing the wisdom of mimicking nature, but today's cities and towns inhibit the four processes through which Nature functions, particularly the mineral and water cycles.

mineral cycle: Nutrients and wastes that cycled for billions of years now accumulate in city dumps or enter our water in such concentration that they create pollution. While nature can break down and cycle a vast array of natural substances, it is not equipped to break down or cycle many of our synthetic chemicals and substances, which accumulate and become a poison to our environment and to us.

water cycle: Today's cities have many impermeable surfaces—roofs, pavements, roads, parking lots and more. These surfaces shed vast amounts of water into our waterways carrying wastes that can neither be broken down nor cycled by nature. Furthermore, they shed billions of gallons of water while we continue to pipe in water at great cost.

Any town or city can mimic nature's mineral and water cycles to an amazing degree with nothing but increased profitability to businesses and reduced costs to the city or town. Cisterns can catch vast amounts of clean water off roofs for use in homes. City developers can construct pavements, parking lots and roads of porous blocks and use other creative practices that help water soak into the ground. Roads can be periodically sprayed with oil-eating bacteria to prevent underground pollution. Enormous savings can be made in energy and water use by very simple techniques once there is an awareness of how important it is and how much more profit these techniques can generate than today's short term decisions and practices.

Likewise, where your city lies on the brittleness scale matters. Planning and regulations that result in a city being surrounded by 10- to 15-acre homesites do not cause environmental damage if the city is fairly nonbrittle and soil is almost impossible to expose. The same cannot be said of cities in brittle environments, such as Albuquerque, Los Angeles, or Phoenix. If these cities are surrounded by 10- to 15-acre homesites, inevitably damage is done because most of the ground between plants will be bare.

Because residents in such "subdivisions" automatically displace any wild herding animals that may have resided there, or have too few or too stationary livestock (horses, goats, etc.), they exacerbate the bare-ground problem. If their animals don't move, plants have no time to recover and regrow, and thus get overgrazed. This in turn exposes more soil. Thus, the challenge for people in those areas is how development can help build a community rather than destroy the land base that sustains it. By knowing what you want to achieve, and how the ecosystem functions, you can determine what policies and actions will help move you in the right direction.

As soil cover is so vital to the security of your future and your wealth, why not go and have a look at land surrounding your city or town. The secret to looking at land is to look down at it and not across it. So as you drive out and pass a farmer's fields full of corn or soybeans that appear to cover 100 percent of the soil, stop and walk into the fields. As you look down into these apparently covered fields, you will generally find that over 50 percent of the ground is bare between the plants—and that can only lead to increasing droughts and/or floods.

If you drive out in the more brittle environments, as for instance between Albuquerque and Santa Fe, you will pass miles of grassland and shrubs with apparently good ground cover as you look across the landscape. Once more, stop and take a short walk. You will generally see that well over 80 percent of the soil is bare due to the way the land and animals are managed. Also, you will begin to understand that the policies advocated by some of our most important environmental organizations on such lands—for example, removing livestock from public lands, using fire to reduce the amount of dead and/or dry vegetation—would likely worsen the situation.

Knowing this much, you can begin to see how your daily decisions about what you buy, how you dispose of it, whether you support recycling efforts, and what you vote for in regard to town policies and programs, all affect you and your children's welfare.

You can make a difference. In fact the only way to improve you own life, your family's life as well as that of your community and beyond, is through the decisions you make each day. Like the previous examples, our choices as consumers and citizens impact agricultural producers, politicians, and policy. So whether, you support agricultural producers raising range-fed meat (beef, chicken, lamb, etc.) or organic produce grown under regenerative practices, or work to support the efforts of people (in whatever walk of life) who want to create a healthy environment rather than protect or conserve a severely damaged one, your knowledge of the four ecosystem processes is essential to making good decisions.

Every one of us makes decisions in our own self-interest. Unfortunately, we often don't realize that those decisions generally do not support our self-interest other than in the short term. But if we keep in mind the way the ecosystem functions, and how our decisions might affect its ability to function, we can increase not only our current quality of life, but also that of future generations. Like those small drops of rain that become floods, our decisions will collectively change our world.

conclusion

With the basic understanding of Holistic Management and the ecosystem processes under your belt, you now have a foundation for making the most of the Holistic Management decision-making process. Remember that the water cycle, mineral cycle, energy flow, and community dynamics are merely different aspects of the same thing—our ecosystem as it functions. When any one of these processes is not functioning well, we compromise our health and financial stability and that of future generations. Given an understanding of these processes, and an awareness of the role our decisions play in enhancing or diminishing their health, we can work to create an environment for future generations of which we can feel proud.

Kids' Capacity

When we test our decisions, everyone's ideas are valued, which has been instrumental in continuing to foster strong relationships, especially with our two sons who are eleven and nine years old. As we've evolved in our practice of Holistic Management, we've seen the boys show more ownership and responsibility toward our holisticgoal. They make it come alive by bringing diversity of ideas and play into our planning. Their capacity for creativity and lateral-thinking cannot be over-emphasized.

Peter and Karen Woodward

Farmers
Wickepin, Western Australia

3

aye aye, captain

getting the most from your crew

One of the major benefits of Holistic Management is how it helps people make decisions both as individuals and as groups. Because Holistic Management encourages collaborative decision-making, it can help groups achieve more from their team members when they incorporate it with the other decision-making, conflict resolution, or planning processes they currently use. But doing anything effectively in a group takes good communication skills. That's why many people have found that increasing their ability to communicate (particularly, their ability to listen and structure discussions so everyone really does participate) before they begin forming their holisticgoal, helps them get the most out of their discussions. Other people have also found that assessing their current situation helps them know what they need to improve as part of the goal-setting, decision-making, or planning processes.

So the first step in making the most of your crew is to assess your current communication styles and see if you can use some improvement. The second step is to determine your current abilities so you have some sense of your resources as a group before you actually set sail with the Holistic Management process. By simultaneously learning or improving your teamwork and communication skills, you can increase your ability to make the most of Holistic Management.

the importance of communication in decision-making

When you form a holisticgoal and test decisions as a group, you will discover that the more you listen to each other and understand what motivates each individual in the group, the more you accomplish because you are pulling together as a team. For example, if five really intelligent people work in a group, they can produce great things working alone, lousy results if they can't work together, and fantastic results if they can collaborate and build on each other's skills. In fact, most of the problems we have today are people problems not technology or resource problems. When people can't work together or are in conflict over resource use or management decisions, then we often focus on the resource or management issues as the problem rather than the way people are interacting.

language and reality

We affect or influence our capacity by the language we use. Many studies have shown that the language or words we use create the reality we see or experience, and, perhaps more importantly, how our children experience life. And, consciously choosing our words forces us to be more conscious about our thoughts, which is half the fun.

In other words, we can change our frame of reference by the language we use. So when you think about framing sentences in a different way, you not only change your attitude, but you also ask a different set of questions or look for new clues. And if you do that, you are more likely to really look at the bigger picture and consider all the possibilities. People can spend an inordinate amount of time finding the right answer to the wrong question because they have allowed their language to shape their reality. See the exercise "Asking the Right Questions" (a3-1) in Appendix 1.

Leadership is action, not position.
—Donald H. McGannon

exercise 3-1.

language and reality.

purpose:

identifying our language patterns

Below is a list of phrases adapted from a list in Susan Jeffers' *Feel the Fear and Do It Anyway*. Look over each column and see which phrases you use most often (or which phrases other people in your group think you use). Which category do you tend to use more? Which ones would be the easiest to change? How could you change them?

Reactive Language	Proactive Language
I can't	I won't
I should	I could
It's not my fault	I'm responsible
It's a problem	It's an opportunity
I'm never satisfied	I want to learn and grow
Life's a struggle	Life's an adventure/game
I hope/I wish	I'll try/I will
If only	Next time
What will I do?	I'll do the best I can
It's terrible	It's a learning experience
I have to	I get to
This always happens	What can I do differently?
When?	Plan now
I'm scared	I'm also excited
You did this to me	I had a piece in this

communication and the art of listening

Bob Chadwick, a nationally known facilitator of consensus-building workshops says, "There's a reason we were given two ears and one mouth." Like many professionals in the conflict resolution field, he believes that miscommunication occurs because people don't feel heard or listened to, not because they are unable to express their thoughts clearly.

If you listen to someone only to gain information that you can refute, then you will ask quite different questions of that person than if you wanted to understand why he felt the way he did. Likewise, your conclusions about that person will be vastly different. And if someone doesn't feel heard, you can bet he isn't going to spend much energy trying to hear you. For an additional exercise on listening and empathy, see "Points of View" (a3-2) in Appendix 1.

| **exercise 3-2.**

consensus-building process

purpose:

a way to give everyone a chance to speak and feel heard | This exercise follows the basic structure that Bob Chadwick uses when he facilitates a consensus-building workshop.

1) Ask everyone involved in a project, meeting, planning, etc. (including yourself) to answer the following questions:

a)   How do you feel about this situation or issue?

b)   What would be the worst outcome of this situation?

c)   What would be the best outcome of this situation?

d)   What are the behaviors and beliefs necessary to create the best possible outcome?

e)   What strategies and actions will you commit to doing to create the best possible outcome?

2) Take turns answering the questions one at a time. Go around in a circle until everyone has had a chance to answer the first question, then go on to the next. People can pass if they wish. Write down everyone's answers verbatim and make sure you have recorded them correctly.

3) Read each of the statement's recorded out loud.

4) Do not give any comments or feedback.

Chadwick's process encourages everyone to speak and feel heard. When people see their words written down verbatim and read aloud with no criticism or discussion, then others feel free to speak their minds. You ask the questions in a specific sequence to get issues and agendas out into the open, and find out what people's worst fears are so that they can then express what they want. Once people speak those thoughts and feelings, they can determine what would help create their best possible outcome and what they're willing to do to make it happen. |

assessing capacity

Holistic Management, and tools such as consensus-building, are processes you can use every day. As you begin to explore your current situation and think more deeply about how you would like your life to be now and in the future, you will notice many patterns and structures that you hadn't noticed before. Your habits and current skills are your current capacity. How you make decisions, how you act on those decisions, how you structure your family or participate in it, how you communicate with one another and what you think about each other and the world around you (whether consciously or not) will all impact what you choose to see, how you choose to respond to people and situations, and your attitude about those events.

People in a group are often at different stages in their lives. As you begin to work as a collaborative team pulling together toward a common goal, you will learn that everyone is a leader or can offer your team unique skills. But they must feel committed to the work at hand and feel a part of the process. Don't expect that kind of immediate involvement from everyone at the start. However, as you increase your capacity to learn, grow, and "walk your talk," those around you will respond. In other words, if you focus on improving yourself and the environment or structure of the group, rather than individuals within the group, you will have a far greater impact on increasing the group's capacity to meet and exceed their needs.

intelligences and making the most of your group

Every head is a world.
—Cuban proverb

The more you recognize what each family member has to offer, and the more you engage those talents and skills, the more you will produce what you want to produce. Understanding that various intelligences (whether verbal, musical, artistic, spatial, physical, or interpersonal) do exist is the first step. In *Multiple Intelligences,* Howard Gardner describes these different intelligences and what each type of person brings to the table.

While people possess various levels of these different intelligences, if you want to engage everyone in your group, you need to offer different ways of exploring a topic or idea to increase participation. (For example, a visually oriented person may need

Not In Front of the Children

The other day I found myself saying to my kids, "I have to go to a meeting." I started noticing the words the other adults in our community were using in conjunction with such words as work and family obligations. We talked together and realized what kind of message we were giving to the kids, that we were doing these things out of obligation or guilt rather than out of a sense of choice or desire, which isn't true. Now I make sure that I tell my kids, "I get to go to a meeting," and it helps to remind me of all the truth in that statement.

Shannon Horst
Executive Director, Center for Holistic Management
Albuquerque, New Mexico

visual diagrams during a discussion.) And you will have a better sense of what each person can contribute to the group if you recognize diversity of thought and interests as a strength and asset rather than a hindrance.

You can engage everyone when you recognize their individual strengths and use them in the various group activities. For example, if some people in your group have strong analytical skills, then use those skills in the exercises. Some people, especially men, have difficulty expressing feelings because they haven't developed that skill. However, they might have had a great deal of practice with analytical skills. If you can involve people at a level in which they feel comfortable, then you can introduce some new skills or ideas that may stretch them out of their comfort zone. In this way the group can help each team member strengthen old skills or gain new ones.

In fact, many people have found the Holistic Management process helpful because it can balance those skills that may be stronger in one gender (or individual) more than the other due to social influences (i.e., the analytical left brain for men and intuitive right brain for women). Such predominance in one hemisphere in the brain is not

Extended Family

We hold regular meetings where all family members are considerably more involved in decision-making than they had ever been before we started practicing Holistic Management. Everyone is encouraged to talk. Our extended family numbers 28 people which includes my 87 year-old mother, my sister and her husband, our children, their spouses, grandchildren, nieces, nephews and their families.

These meetings are sometimes confrontational, but because everyone is encouraged to express their feelings, we all feel that our desires and interests have value and, if not shared, they are at least respected. Is it easy? Definitely not! However, we have learned through Holistic Management that in order to go fast, you must first go slow.

The result, in our immediate family, has been astounding. Our children are combining their labor and enthusiasm in developing the "resort"—a dwelling on our land that is being established and shared by them when they visit the ranch on weekends and holidays.

I guess the bottom line is that Holistic Management has brought our family together in a way that probably would not have happened before. Our children have a warm respect for one another and have developed feelings of love, ownership and responsibility for the ultimate destiny of our (their) home.

Bill Burrows

Retired college professor
Red Bluff, California

necessarily genetic, but the point is that everyone usually has a dominant hemisphere or way of thinking or making decisions. The Holistic Management process includes testing questions that help people who use one style of thinking/feeling more than another for decision-making to make more complete use of their brainpower. It can also become a common language from which both parties can speak.

For example, an analytical person can learn how to pay attention to the emotional aspects of a decision through some of the testing questions or through the goal setting that encourages discussion about feelings. If another person is more intuitive or feeling, then he can learn how to integrate some of the more analytical parts of decision-making when using the testing questions that require some thought and research to back up intuitive decisions. Through incorporating all these strengths as a group, or encouraging a diversity of perspectives, people can make better decisions and/or resolve conflict that might have arisen because both parties thought their way was the only right way.

(For more information on BrainStyles™, see Marlane Miller's book, *BrainStyles: Change Your Life Without Changing Who You Are.*)

leadership by example

You can't depend on your judgment when your imagination is out of focus.

—*Mark Twain*

If you have decided to "lead" your family in practicing Holistic Management, then you have to make sure that everyone is engaged in the process as much as possible so that they will have ownership in the results. It isn't always possible to get everyone's involvement, but keep asking and thinking of new ideas to involve more people in the process. After all, their lack of engagement might only be a symptom of a larger issue (see the Cause and Effect test in Chapter Five).

Luckily, there are no mistakes, only insights, so if all else fails, forge ahead on your own. Your modeling (acting the way you would like others to behave) and growth will ultimately draw the curious around you. "Your Turn" (a3-3) is another exercise that you can play as a game with your family or use as a training exercise to help promote appreciation and use of the different intelligences each member possesses. (See Appendix 1).

Osmosis Leadership

Trying to get our kids to sit down and help formulate a goal did not work for us. We found that as we started practicing Holistic Management the children learned it by osmosis and they gradually started to participate more and more. We also used the holistic decision-making process to help our children sort out their problems. In these situations, we've led them through the process using examples and exploring possibilities. That way they could learn to go through the same process on their own when they are ready.

Ian and Pam Mitchell Innes

Farmers
Natal, South Africa

conclusion

Making the most of your crew can take some effort if you aren't used to really communicating or appreciating the different skills that everyone brings to the table. Before you begin the Holistic Management goal-setting process, take the time to learn effective communication skills if you don't already have them. If you can learn how to work as an effective team now before you begin the process, you will have an even greater head start on moving toward the life that you want to create.

Nothing is so contagious as an example.
—De La Roche Foucauld

<u>Decisions, Decisions</u>

I think that Holistic Management can really help parents learn to talk with their children in a new way. Some parents think they are talking to their children when they are lecturing them or giving them directions. But with Holistic Management, you find out what your kids think and feel and where they want to go and how you can incorporate that into the family structure. It really helps to get people to a different level of conversation no matter what relationship they have.

Men can be scared of intimacy whether with their partners or their children. I've talked to some of my male friends about the conversations I have with my wife and they tell me they could never talk like that. They don't even allow themselves to think that deeply much less express it. But with Holistic Management you start looking at yourself so you can start thinking about those things and then be better able to listen to others talk about their thoughts. By getting deeper with yourself you can get deeper with others and that brings depth to your life.

Robert Pasztor

High School Teacher
Albuquerque, New Mexico

Nothing has a stronger influence psychologically on their environment, and especially on their children, than the unlived life of their parents.

—Carl Jung

A New Place

I think men in this society are brought up to take action and to be self-reliant. They don't necessarily think holistically. In some ways, I think women understand Holistic Management more intuitively because they are more comfortable with feelings and discussing them.

The hardest part of Holistic Management for me is creating a shared goal. In the past, I wanted to go out and just do something. But I realized that by default I couldn't do everything I want to alone. And if I want to get it done, I have to work with a team. And if you are working with a team, it's critical to remember that you can only go as fast as the slowest member. Sure I could crank out spreadsheets, but it was hard to listen to people's hopes and feelings.

But it has gotten easier for me. I realized you have to change patterns if you want to get to some place new. Having the Holistic Management framework helped me because it provides an avenue of expression for everyone and a chance to integrate that information in a real and positive way.

Drausin Wulsin

Grass-based dairy farmer
Cincinnati, Ohio

4

building your ship

defining the whole

Before you set out on your journey, you must build your ship from what you have at your disposal, your knowledge of the type of ship you want to sail, and where you want to sail. After all, if you sail a schooner, you will have a far different task with different needs and resources than if you sail a dinghy. In other words, if you don't consider *what* you want to manage you can end up with a host of problems later.

Defining the whole is the first step in the Holistic Management goal setting process. This step essentially lays the foundation of what you want to manage by setting the parameters for the decisions you make. The

key concepts for this chapter

decision-makers

resource base

money

Sorting Out the Whole

Holistic Management introduced the concept of looking at our lives as a whole. When some of our adult children returned home to help with the family business, we had many adults with individual backgrounds and experiences starting out on a multifaceted work and living experience. So it was important for us all to start from the firm foundation of understanding that we could not get hung up on parts but must plan and work always with the whole in mind if we were going to succeed as a business and be happy as a family.

It was and is inspiring to us to realize that we can go beyond old paradigms of thinking and draw upon our creative juices to solve challenges in new ways. With so many people involved in our day to day activities, and a lot of "bosses," we are so happy to have a common list of questions to ask ourselves when a decision needs to be made.

Kay James

Co-owner of James Ranch
Durango, Colorado

---

three components to consider in defining the whole are: the decision-makers involved, the resource base at their disposal, and the money available to them. If you spend time determining what falls into each of these categories in your particular situation, you will have far greater success in achieving the results you want.

For example, many of us waste time trying to control something beyond our control. Or we don't get the commitment from others for a project we want to undertake because we haven't determined ahead of time who needs to help make decisions or be involved with planning. Likewise, if you don't have a clear picture of the resources available to you, you either won't make the most of them or consider how they impact you or you influence them.

This is a good time to inventory all your assets, to take stock of your current situation. While you may discover some liabilities as part of this inventory, don't put that information here. You will, however, use those insights later as you begin to develop your holisticgoal and test the decisions that will take you toward it.

decision-makers

Look at the top diagram on the facing page. In the section labeled *Decision Makers*, you see listed some sample answers to these questions:

- Who makes the decisions?
- Who might help make the decisions some of the time or who has veto power?

While this might seem like a simple exercise, consider the number of families who allow their children no role in decision-making or even in discussions of family "policy." Moreover, many family businesses include adult children who have no more say as adults than they did as children. Likewise, family businesses can have employees outside the family that have no decision-making power. All of these dynamics, especially if they are never discussed, can lead to discontent, lack of productivity, and, in the case of children, rebellion.

resource base

(People and Things)

Now look at the next section of the whole. To determine who or what your resource base includes, consider the following questions.

- Who influences our decisions?
- Whom do we rely on?
- Whom do we affect or influence?
- What major possessions do we have that we can use or rely on?

Many people have a far greater resource base than they realize, or perhaps care to think about. But if you really do understand who and what you rely on and influence, then you have a much better chance of making decisions that include the bigger picture and not just one piece of it.

Tell me, I'll forget. Show me, I may remember. But involve me and I'll understand.

—Chinese proverb

When we quit thinking primarily about ourselves and our own self-preservation, we undergo a truly heroic transformation of consciousness.

—Joseph Campbell

One family's whole

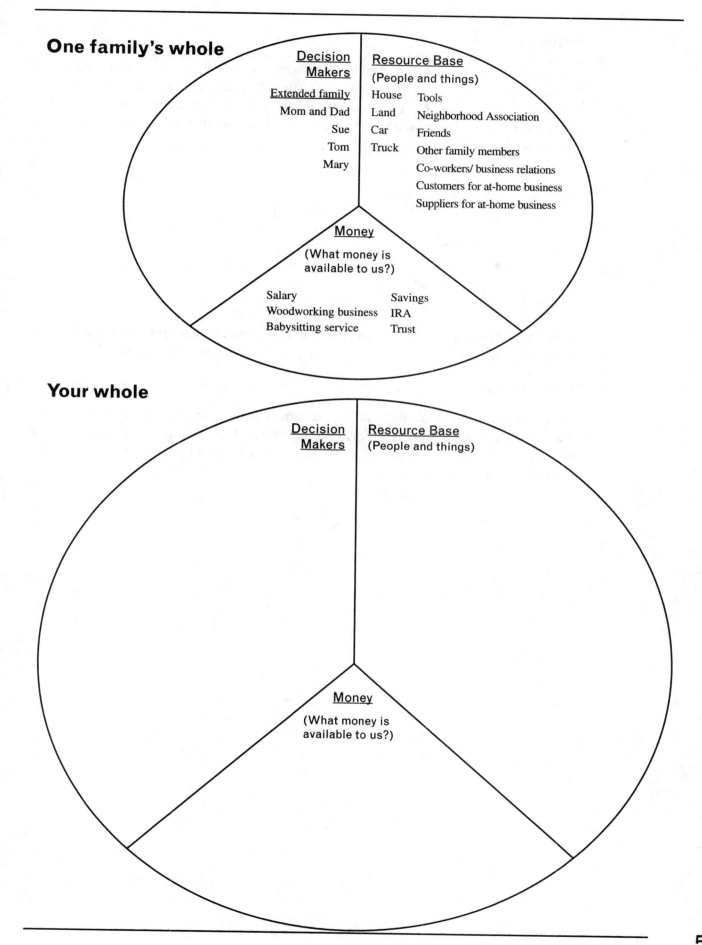

Decision Makers

Extended family
Mom and Dad
Sue
Tom
Mary

Resource Base
(People and things)

House
Land
Car
Truck

Tools
Neighborhood Association
Friends
Other family members
Co-workers/ business relations
Customers for at-home business
Suppliers for at-home business

Money

(What money is available to us?)

Salary
Woodworking business
Babysitting service

Savings
IRA
Trust

Your whole

Decision Makers

Resource Base
(People and things)

Money

(What money is available to us?)

money

While money is obviously part of your resource base, it helps to keep it separate so you can consider all the possible sources. After all, like it or not, money (or financial stability) will greatly affect your ability to live the life you want. You will need to determine all the sources of money that you have so that when you create your financial plan you'll know what you can draw on.

- Income
- Savings
- Bank
- Friends
- Family
- Investments
- Inventory

Now, in the blank space provided, define the whole you are managing, who the decision makers are, what your resource base is, and what money you have available to you.

conclusion

Remember, defining the whole helps you know what you are managing, what you can draw from, and who must help form the holisticgoal. If you can figure that out now while you are not in the midst of a crisis, you will be able to make better use of that information and those resources.

Whose Goal?

Initially our breakdown came in developing a goal that we both bought into. It was hard for us to have a goal that enveloped all of the facets of our business and family life. Once that was addressed, the practice of Holistic Management was simplified enough that it has seemed easy since then.

I think the reason for this breakdown was our egos. I admit that my ego was involved in what I wanted out of the goal rather than finding a better, third solution. My perception is that my husband wanted the goal to only take in his part of our business when the business facets of my life (art) were not considered part of the whole. When both of us finally agreed that what I did was part of the whole, then creating a goal that was both of ours was much easier.

Cheryl Cosner

Artist and livestock producer
Centerville, Washington

Making Decisions with the Whole in Mind

As an adult child coming home with my husband to raise our children in a rural environment around my family of origin, I didn't want us to feel like we were just working for my parents. But with Holistic Management, we have the tools to decide if we want to work for the family and receive a salary, or work with the family and have equity invested in the different enterprises. It also has made a huge difference in the way that decisions are made, mostly that the patriarch of the family doesn't have to bear the pressure of making all the decisions and then listening to all of us complain about the decision if we don't agree. In other words, Holistic Management forces each of us to be responsible for communicating when a decision is needed when it affects the whole.

Jennifer Wheeling

Durango, Colorado

exercise 4-1.

mindmapping
your whole

purpose:

what is our
"whole"

Look at the sample mindmap on the following page to see what a mindmap can look like. This exercise will show you how you influence or are influenced by the whole you have defined. In the empty space below the example, map out your family's whole (or any other whole that you might be trying to manage—business, community, individual, etc.).

(A Note on Mindmapping: Tony Buzan developed this technique, which many people find useful especially when working with holistic processes, like writing or planning. Mindmapping creates an opportunity for the right brain to explore associations among the various ideas that may come to mind during a given exercise. While some people can come to similar conclusions when using a list of ideas, using mindmapping gives a higher probability of seeing things more deeply or seeing connections more clearly.
With mindmapping you simply start with an idea, then associate ideas in any direction, adding more associations as you branch out. Instead of having a list of words, you now have an understanding of the connection between the ideas. For another example of this concept, see the "Holism Exercise" (a1-2) in Appendix 1.)

1) Put anyone that is a decisionmaker in the bubble in the middle of the page. (Decision makers are those who are currently making decisions, have veto power, or who make decisions within the whole at least some of the time—in a family that might include children or elderly parents).

2) Now, list all the resources (people or assets) available to you on a separate piece of paper, or just start weaving them into the mindmap you are creating. When you do this, make sure you draw lines between the bubbles to show the relationship or connections between the various resources.

3) Consider who and what you already have that are important to you and to the quality of life for the whole you are managing. Think about who or what contributes to your emotional, financial, physical, social, intellectual, spiritual, and aesthetic well-being. Also think about all those who impact you or are impacted by you. These are additional resources you have in your resource base.

The purpose of this exercise is to help you define what it is you are managing and to recognize what resources you, as an individual or as a family, already have that you can use to increase the quality of life. This exercise also helps you realize all of the resources that you affect or can influence. The mind map helps you see what resources are most important in your life, which ones you have more control over than others, and which ones affect you the most. This is important information to remember when you are making plans and decisions later.

A sample mindmap of a whole.

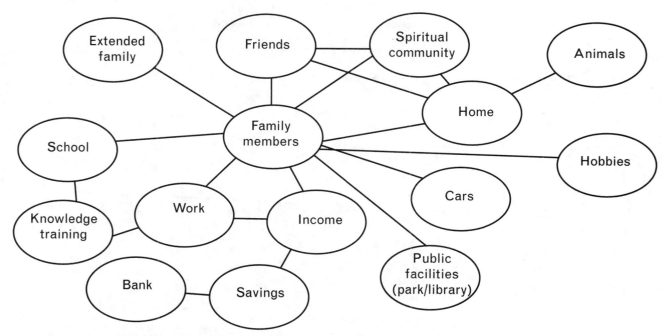

Our mindmap of a whole.

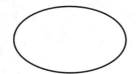

Sticking With It

It took about two years and a couple of tries before our family developed a holisticgoal that had meaning for everyone. I had to practically squeeze input out of the other family members. I also made the mistake of paraphrasing what they did say. Much to my surprise, it had no meaning to anyone but me! A year later, we did something different. I asked my family members a series of questions over several months and collected their written responses. The questions had to do with what was important to them, what they enjoyed, what they wanted, etc. I used their exact words in the holisticgoal. When it was read for the first time, faces lit up when they heard their own words, values, and dreams. We actually started making plans that day to clean up the yard and to plan for vacations. It has been a reminder that life can be better.

Sandy Matheson

Holistic Management® Certified Educator
Bellingham, Washington

choosing a destination

setting a holisticgoal

Once you've defined your whole, it's time to form your holisticgoal. Make sure you include all the decision makers you listed in your whole. If you include everyone in the goal-setting process, then they will have ownership in the holisticgoal you create as a group and the decisions you make afterwards to move you toward what you describe within it.

A holisticgoal includes three necessary components: quality of life, forms of production, and the future resource base.

When you form your holisticgoal, make sure you complete each step in the order listed because each section builds off the previous one. As you think of new things you want to include, you can certainly add them as your holisticgoal evolves. Many families find that once they have the common ground of a holisticgoal established, they are better able to make decisions and follow through with actions to move them toward what they have described in their holisticgoal.

forming a holisticgoal

The key to forming a holisticgoal is to just do it. Get something down on paper (write it down or talk to someone and have them write it down) so that you can test decisions toward that vision. If you know yourself well enough to know that you won't do anything if you have to sit down all day, then don't design your goal-setting session that way. Develop your holisticgoal in fun, small chunks. Add to what you've already created.

Your holisticgoal will begin to evolve into a more permanent, and more specific, goal as you deepen the trust level among team members and they gain the confidence to risk sharing what is important to them. Crisis situations also tend to move the holisticgoal from general to specific. When you have to make major decisions, you will want to return to your holisticgoal to aid you in finalizing them. If your holisticgoal lacks the detail that you need to help make a decision, you must discern what you must add to address the immediate situation.

quality of life

Quality of life is a catch-all phrase these days, but basically it means what gives your life meaning. We may think: "A new car would make me

key concepts in this chapter

forming a holisticgoal

quality of life

forms of production

future resource base

The most exhausting thing in life, I have discovered, is being insincere.

—Anne Morrow Lindbergh

happy." "A video game would make me happy." "A new relationship would make me happy." Unfortunately, the likelihood of those things bringing happiness for any extended length of time is pretty slim. The odds are more likely that the happiness or sense of fulfillment you feel from such external factors would dwindle rapidly. But if you think about what you hope to gain from those things (i.e. freedom, entertainment, prestige, companionship, romance, etc.) then you are closer to knowing what makes you happy and what you want. As you develop this section of your holisticgoal, think about such areas of your life as economic well-being, relationships, challenge and growth, and purpose and contribution.

Studies demonstrate that no matter what socio-economic income bracket you are in, only a third of the people in each bracket are happy or feel good about their lives. These studies show that it doesn't matter how much money you make or how many possessions you own. Those things don't guarantee happiness. Knowing what they truly value and living a life that allows them to contribute to what they think is important, makes people feel good about their lives. In other words, they know what they want, and how they want to contribute, and they integrate that mission in their lives through their decisions and actions.

Find what you really care about, then live a life that shows it.

—Kate Wolf

So this section of the holisticgoal is to determine what you want in your life as a family, or whatever entity your whole encompasses, like health, financial security, meaningful work, good relationships or whatever else is important to you. Quality of life statements usually look something like this:

- We want good health.
- We want to be debt-free
- We want meaningful and enjoyable friendships and relationships
- We want to be productive
- We want to have fun

Look and you will find it—what is unsought will go undetected.

—Irwin Edman

forms of production

Once you discern what you want, you need to determine what you have to produce to create the quality of life you just described. That's why we call this section the Forms of Production. In some ways this section is the most challenging because you have to think about what you would have to create to make the life you want possible.

For some people, that means looking at underlying beliefs and behaviors that affect the life they want. While this exploration provides a focal point, they must still look at what they have to produce, not how they have to produce it. Once you get into the "hows," you may have conflict as you move away from the common ground you want to establish.

For others, this section is also a time to determine what they must be willing to do—their commitment to creating the life they want. When a group takes the time to write down these ideas and make them public, some amazing shifts happen.

If you feel stuck trying to determine what you need to produce to create the quality of life you want, consider the following question: "What don't we have now or what aren't we doing now, that prevents us from achieving these things we say we want in our Quality of Life?" Take each item in your quality of life statement and determine what you are currently doing and would like to do more consistently.

Examples of Forms of Production statements would be:

Quality of life	Forms of Production
We want balanced lives.	Good time management
We want good communication.	An open, safe, and nonjudgmental environment for communication
We want financial stability	Produce "profit" from meaningful work

The Evolving Goal

By far the biggest influence on the evolution of our holisticgoal was the decisions we tested toward it. If we couldn't arrive at a clear answer when asking the testing guideline questions, we usually found that our goal wasn't yet specific enough.

Once when we were testing whether to buy cattle with borrowed funds or to use someone else's cattle for custom grazing on our ranch, both enterprises passed—one was neither better nor worse than the other. It wasn't until we clarified our holisticgoal and put in the phrase, "We want to be debt free" that it became very clear that buying cattle failed because it did not take us toward our holisticgoal.

Once we made our holisticgoal more specific, it became easier to prioritize our commitments and to drop those that weren't important. Life immediately became more enjoyable. We found, for instance, that in doing our financial planning, we now had the funds for the education and travel that were so important to our quality of life.

Without a holisticgoal, we had no way of knowing whether our actions were taking us in the direction we wanted to go, because we didn't have a direction. Living without a holisticgoal is like having a wind-up toy that changes direction when it hits a wall, or tips over and wastes energy spinning its wheels in the air. We only have a short time on this earth and for the majority of it, we want our wheels on the ground taking us in the direction we want to go.

Don and Randee Halladay
Holistic Management® Certified Educators/Ranchers
Rocky Mountain House, Alberta, Canada

(Excerpted from Holistic Management: A New Framework for Decision-Making) by Allan Savory with Jody Butterfield

future resource base

You won't help anyone if you create the quality of life you want then can't sustain it. In fact, many people won't try to create the quality of life they want because they are afraid they can't sustain it. But you can make decisions that will lead to the quality of life you want and sustain it for generations to come. This concept is like the great law of the Iroquois Confederacy, which states, "In our every deliberation, we must consider the impact of our decisions on the next seven generations." If you can describe what that future must look like (your future resource base), you will make decisions that sustain what you must produce to create the quality of life you want now far into the future.

The future resource base that you describe relates to the resource base you defined in your whole. If you want to sustain that resource base, then you must consider what it needs to look like and how you fit into it. In this section you can describe your future resource base in any way that makes sense to you, but at the very minimum include the following:

- How you must be perceived by the people in your resource base to sustain what you want to produce. You must describe how others in your resource base must see you far into the future so that those people (whether suppliers, clients, friends, community members, or extended family) will continue to support you, respect you, and be loyal to you.

- What the land surrounding your community must be like—healthy, thriving, etc.

- What your community needs to be like.

(Both the community and the surrounding land aren't something you can manage directly as a family, but your decisions will impact their management, which is why you need to describe them. With that picture in mind, you will have a better sense of how your decisions will help support the future resource base you want.)

So, some sample future resource base statements would be:

- We will live in a thriving community with a stable population and adequate public services.

- We will have beautiful and productive land surrounding us, where all four ecosystem processes—water and mineral cycles, energy flow, and community dynamics—are healthy.

- We will be perceived by our community, family, and co-workers as thoughtful, patient, honest, intelligent, funny, resourceful, and having good work ethics.

- We will have abundant natural resources that we use/manage sustainably.

conclusion

In the next few pages are a few exercises for either forming a holisticgoal or aiding in the introspection that helps to clarify what you want in the whole you are managing now and into the future. There are also additional exercises (a5-1 to a5-3) in Appendix 1. For many, putting down the thoughts that make up a holisticgoal can be the most difficult and rewarding act they have ever done. With a clear sense of what you want and what you need to do to produce and sustain it, you have a compass to guide every decision.

Saying What You Want

I think the biggest problem that people have with setting a holistic-goal is when they are frightened of what it might tell them. We know of several situations where if the people were really honest with themselves, they wouldn't even be in the profession they are in. If you have been a rancher or lawyer or accountant for 30 years and know that if you really were honest you would rather not be doing that work, what else do you do? It is easier not to look too deeply and just carry on the way you are. This is particularly negative if there are families involved. For example, the children become the excuse—"I have been battling here all my life just for you." And if the children aren't that keen on that occupation, they feel pressured into helping in the family business. We feel that it is critical that children (particularly teenagers) are part of the holisticgoal setting so that everyone can be open about what they want in life, and that family members can support each other.

Dick and Judy Richardson

Holistic Management® Certified Educators Vorna Valley, South Africa

Family Investment

Holistic Management International told us it took the average family two years to really get a "complete" holisticgoal. That was hard to believe for such a simple process...and besides I had already set the goal on my trip back from my first Holistic Management workshop.

To make a long story short, it took us three years to produce our written holistic-goal, but in the process we discovered a great deal about our situation and ourselves.

The first thing we found was that even though we have a good family life, we didn't communicate as well as we should (starting with my wife and myself). This was the beginning of a search to improve our own skills as well as to acquire some new ones to improve our relationships as a couple and family. We tried a number of processes and techniques, and learning them cost more than some people might feel is necessary to spend on something that is not broken (i.e. I have a good marriage). Yet many of us find it easy to spend plenty upgrading possessions. We have found that investments in self-improvement and relationships are very cost effective! Think about what a divorce can cost.

George Work

Rancher and speaker San Miguel, California

A Sample holisticgoal

(Written by a middle-aged couple to create the life they want)

Quality of Life

To be engaged in meaningful work for the rest of our lives, and to be excited and enthusiastic about what we have to do and get to do each day. To be secure financially, physically and emotionally into old age; to be known for our honor, integrity, chivalry and spirit. To maintain robust health and physical stamina; to enjoy an abundance of mutually satisfying relationships. To explore and experience wild places, and to ensure those places will still be there when our grandchildren's grandchildren seek to find them. To live simply, and consume sparingly.

What We Have To Produce (Forms of Production)

* Profit from meaningful work.

* Work or leisure time in wild places.

* Time for learning, meaningful discussion, companionship and exercise.

* A warm and hospitable home environment—wherever home happens to be at any time—in which friends, family and colleagues always feel welcome.

Future Resource Base

People: We are known to be compassionate and thoughtful, well-informed, good listeners, fun to be with, adventurous, and supportive.

Land: The land surrounding and supporting our town will be stable and productive. Wildlife will be plentiful—we'll be able to see animals, or signs of them anytime we venture out. The river will run clear and be full of life, and eagles will nest in the trees alongside it once again.

From *Holistic Management: A New Framework for Decision-Making* by Allan Savory with Jody Butterfield.

Image creates desire. You will want what you imagine.

—J.G. Gallimore

---

exercise 5-4.

the adjective exercise

purpose:

make conscious the traits you value and how others perceive you

1) Have each group member list at least 10 adjectives describing themselves (funny, smart, kind, etc.).

2) Then have each person take another sheet of paper and write his or her name on the top.

3) Pass these sheets around so that everyone else is now describing someone else.

4) Have them list 10 adjectives for that person, then pass the sheet on to the next person who can place a checkmark next to any adjective they also agree with, as well as adding their own words.

5) When that list is complied, someone else besides the person described reads the list. In the discussion that follows consider the following questions:

- What did you wish was on the list?

- What do you wish wasn't?

- What behaviors are necessary for people to perceive you the way you would like to be perceived?

The purpose of this exercise is to make you aware of the traits you value and how others perceive you. This information can help you define more clearly each section of your holisticgoal.

This exercise is a variation of an exercise in Robert S. Eliot's book, From Stress to Strength.

exercise 5-1.
your holisticgoal

purpose:
creating your first holisticgoal

note: this is just a starting point. use as much space as you need to write out your holisticgoal.

quality of life

forms of production

future resource base

exercise 5-2.
family crest

purpose:

1) to discuss representations of your family

2) produce a visual product that you can put on the refrigerator or some prominent place as a reminder of how you want to be perceived.

This is a good exercise to help you think about how you want to represent your family. The Family Crest (or you can do the family totem pole or whatever art form best fits your culture) is an old idea that helped express noble thoughts and family lineage.

Using the empty form on the next page, create a family crest for your family. If you don't have an artist in the family, you can cut out pictures in magazines or make a color copy of a picture from a book and then trim the copy to fit into the crest. If these pages seem to small, get larger paper to make the crest.

Decide what animals, plants, birds, insects, etc., represent your family based on the traits they possess. For example, one of the squares in our family crest is a bee because bees are a communal insect, each working for the best outcome for the hive and always busy. We also decided on the cedar tree for another square because it is tough and useful and it reminds us of the cedars on our land. The kids can really take charge of and be involved in this exercise.

Make your work to be in keeping with your purpose.

—*Leonardo da Vinci*

Man's capacities have never been measured, nor are we to judge of what he can do by any precedent, so little has been tried.

—*Henry David Thoreau*

Family Crest

**exercise
5-3.**

future
community
brochure

purpose:

to show
what my
community
must be like
to sustain
what I want
to produce

To help you create a vision of what your community must be like to sustain what you want to produce, pretend for a moment that you are in charge of the advertising campaign for your community.

Step One: Get a map of your area. You will need to include the closest city over 25,000 people and everything within a 50-mile radius. This way you will have more of an opportunity to see how other people's decisions might impact you or yours might impact them. It creates an artificial boundary, but gives you a place to start.

Step Two: Once you have your map, look at the scale and decide the distance that 50 miles represents given the scale of the map. Get a compass or a pencil tied to a piece of string. Now put the compass or the piece of string on where you live and make a circle with your pencil. If that circle doesn't include the closest big city, draw a circle around that. Now retrace both those circles with a red pen or marker. Catalog the following features. (If you really like this project or want to make the most of it, go for a series of drives on the weekend and explore your area):

1) List the waterways on the map and where they come from,

2) Create a pie chart that will show the relative sizes of the particular types of land in that area (mountains, deserts, prairies, marshes, forest, etc.). Use percentages to indicate the size of each pie slice.

3) Create a pie chart of how the land is being used (agricultural, residential, industrial, retail, recreational). What percentage does each type of land represent?

4) Identify the community resources that you use or might need to use in the next 100 years including:

    a)   schools and universities

    b)   libraries

    c)   parks, forests, etc.

    d)   businesses

    e)   community services (police, hospital, fire, etc.)

    f)   water

Include in this list the people upon whom you rely in your community.

5) Identify five of your area's greatest strengths (What brought you there or keeps you there?).

6) Identify five of your area's weaknesses or limitations (What makes you think about moving away?). Change these to what needs to be there instead (i.e. if you have poverty in your area, then you might write a statement about needing a healthy and equitable economy)

7) Ask someone elderly in your area who has lived there all her life, what the area used to be like (the people, the work, the weather , the services, etc.)

8) Analyze the information you've collected. You know what you want your life to be like. Will the community and the land surrounding it support what you must produce to create that life? If it won't, what would? List what else you need.

Step Three: Once you have all your ideas down on paper, it's time to create the brochure for your community. Every good brochure needs some graphics to really catch a person's eye. Draw some pictures, copy illustrations or use photographs that help you really show to people outside your area what your area has to offer. As you write the text, remember that this brochure is for the community you have to have to sustain the life you say you want.

setting sail

testing your decisions

Now that you have a holisticgoal and know your destination, you need something to move you toward it. Think of the Holistic Management testing questions as the navigational tools that will guide your journey. As you set sail, you consult your maps, sextant, compass, or the stars. These tools keep you moving toward your chosen destination. Likewise, once you have formed your holisticgoal, the testing questions ensure that each of your decisions continues to move you toward the life you want.

the importance of making conscious decisions

Making decisions can be stressful, especially when you're in a crisis or when you feel the decision is particularly important. And really, every decision is important because our actions can have far-reaching effects. Moreover, while many of us will consider these ramifications when we make decisions, we sometimes aren't consistently rigorous in the way we test or consider the possible results of our decisions.

If you look at how people get "off track" in their lives and wonder where their lives went, it happened one decision at a time. Little decisions can add up to big life changes. Think about a time when you decided to do something different. Maybe it was something as simple as smiling at a child in a grocery store line instead of reading the magazines. How did that decision impact your day? Your life? Think about all the big decisions you've made about where to go to school or live, what you wanted to study or do, whom you wanted to date or marry, or any number of things. It is hard to separate the little decisions that led to that big decision. Can you remember how you made these decisions or what influenced you?

Prior to making a major decision most of us consciously choose to do some research, follow our intuition or instinct, ask for advice, think about past experience or respond out of habit or instinct. And often times, little unconscious decisions can lead us to big unconscious ones that take us in a direction we never intended. It can be tricky to make most of your decisions consciously, but having a holisticgoal makes it easier because you can test your decisions toward the kind of life you have described.

With Holistic Management, you can more consistently make conscious decisions because you have a reason to take that extra effort. If you have a clear picture of where you want to be, then you will weigh your decisions

key concepts in this chapter

the importance of making conscious decisions

how to use the testing questions

cause and effect

sustainability

weak link

marginal reaction

energy/money source and use

society and culture

Testing, Testing

This past summer we used the testing questions to help us make a decision about whether or not to build a larger greenhouse to produce the plant material for the farm. We had a builder design the barn/greenhouse and give us a bid, which came in way over what we thought we were going to have to spend. Granted, he is one of the best builders in the county, but it still blew us away.

So out came the testing questions. We got into it, and in about 15 minutes we were able to tell that the greenhouse violated our quality of life statement so blatantly that we had to just stop the whole notion of building it right now. One of our major insights from testing the decision was that in order to justify the expense, I would have to have the greenhouse producing something to sell all year long. The idea of building the greenhouse took a huge downward spiral then because we decided to take three winter months off after working overtime in the other nine months. We also realized that my husband would have to work longer away from home in order to pay for it, so we instantly knew it was not the right move.

Instead, we decided to take a tenth of the money that we would have spent and buy the necessary equipment for growing all the plants that we need in the garage. We are confident that we can do this and feel so good about the way the whole decision was made that we know we did the right thing.

Jennifer Wheeling
Durango, Colorado

in the context of that picture. If you don't have that bigger picture, then your decision-making can result in shortsighted decisions or decisions that only address short-term needs. Or, if you have conflicting needs, your decisions can be to meet one need to the detriment of another need with no sense of your priorities.

So making sound decisions consistently can be an overwhelming task if you don't have a way of keeping it simple. The Holistic Management testing questions keep it simple. You can play around with the guidelines all you want, but when the crisis arrives, you know that you have something that is tried and true that will help you make a sound decision no matter how many factors seem to be swirling around you. In an increasingly complex world, that's a comforting thought.

how to use the testing questions

Anytime you're ready to make a decision, big or small, think about your holisticgoal and ask yourself the series of testing questions listed below. If it's a complicated situation, put your written holisticgoal in front of you. If the answers to the questions suggest that this decision will move you toward your holisticgoal, then act on it. If the decision doesn't pass most of the tests you figure it: 1) won't work, 2) needs major revamping before it will work, or 3) you are going to do it anyway knowing that you will sooner or later have to address why it didn't pass those tests. If you can't figure out whether or not the decision would pass a test, that either means that you need to get more information or that particular test doesn't apply to this case. In fact, very few decisions involve all the tests.

With holistic decision-making, no one test holds sway over any of the others. When you run a decision through all the testing questions, you now have the big picture from which to make your final decision. You don't have to take the tests in any certain order, but you must end with the society and culture test because that test depends on the picture that emerges from all the other tests. Two exercises to help you practice the testing questions are "The Tester" (a6-1) and "Testing Decisions" (a6-3) in Appendix 1.

the testing questions

cause and effect

Does this action address the root cause of the problem or are you merely treating a symptom of the problem?

sustainability

If you take this action, will it lead toward or away from the future resource base described in your holisticgoal?

weak link

Social

Have you considered and/or addressed any confusion, anger, or opposition this action could create with people whose support you need in the near or distant future?

Biological

In taking this action, are you addressing the weakest point in the life cycle of this organism?

Financial

Does this action strengthen the weakest link in your chain of production?

marginal reaction

Which action provides the greatest return, in terms of your holisticgoal, for the time and/or money you invest?

energy/money, source and use

Is the money or energy used in this action derived from the most appropriate source in terms of your holisticgoal?

Will the way in which it is used lead you toward your holisticgoal?

society and culture

How do you feel about this action now?

Will it lead to the quality of life you desire?

Will it adversely affect the quality of life of others?

> Note: The last test is the Gross Profit Analysis. Because you only use this test in financial decisions, it is included in Chapter Eight, Financial Planning.

One must live the way one thinks or end up thinking the way one has lived.

—Paul Bourget

cause and effect

Does this action address the root cause of the problem or are you merely treating a symptom of the problem?

The cause and effect test is based on the idea that we can often respond to something as if it is the problem when it is merely the symptom of an underlying problem. But the cause and effect test helps you probe deeper until you really get closer to the root problem. In doing so, you then have information to make a sound decision.

We always know that society is full of folly and will deceive us in the matter of humanity. It is an unreliable horse and blind into the bargain. Woe to the driver if he falls asleep.

—Albert Schweitzer

exercise 6-1.
cause and effect

purpose:

practice finding the underlying cause

Sometimes working through a cause and effect problem can be tricky. Because such a problem requires some persistence and curiosity don't wait until you feel stressed or are in the middle of the problem to explore the possibilities. Instead, if you practice this skill more as a game, you can apply what you've learned more easily in the thick of things. This can be a good exercise to do around the dinner table. Use the example on the facing page as a starting point.

Pick something that everyone can discuss (a family issue or pattern that isn't too loaded so people won't get defensive). You don't want to start with a world problem unless everyone can contribute. Use the example to the right to spark ideas, then use the blank sample on the following page to help monitor your own discussion. Often you will find that what you thought was the problem is really more of an indicator or symptom of other deeper problems. If you address the root cause of those problems, many of them will vanish without further effort on your part. However, you might need to make an immediate decision to alleviate the situation while you work on the long-term solution.

Another variation of this exercise is called the "Five Why's," which Peter Senge discusses in his book, *The Fifth Discipline Fieldbook*. In this exercise, when you explore the reason for a problem you ask "Why?" each time that you provide an answer. See if you can go back at least five layers from your initial answer to the first "why." If you aren't at the root cause by then, you're a lot closer than you were. This type of questioning is also called acting like a two-year-old.

Don't worry if you aren't sure that you've really determined the root cause, because if nothing else, you've thought more deeply. In the example to the right, there are many other factors, and each case would be unique. As in the example, just by doing the exercise, the focus has shifted from Sam being the problem to understanding that Sam is just an indicator of a bigger problem. He's like the canaries that miners once used to warn them of gas leaks in the mine. A dead canary was an indicator of a larger problem (gas leak). Sam's behavior is a clue to other family members that something needs to change.

Immediate decision: **Give Sam food before dinner so he can enjoy social time at dinner**

Long-term decision: **Get job training**

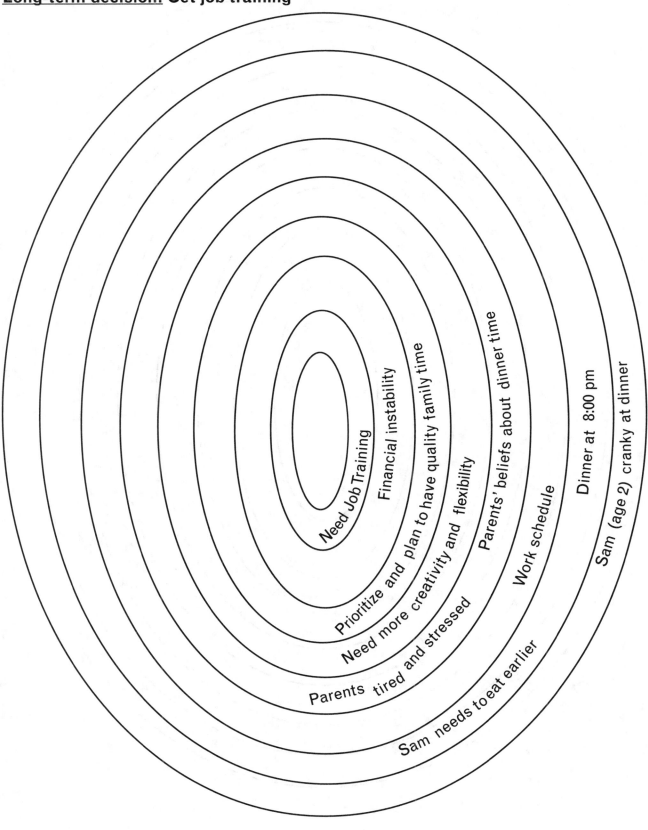

Need Job Training

Financial instability

Prioritize and plan to have quality family time

Need more creativity and flexibility

Parents' beliefs about dinner time

Parents tired and stressed

Work schedule

Dinner at 8:00 pm

Sam needs to eat earlier

Sam (age 2) cranky at dinner

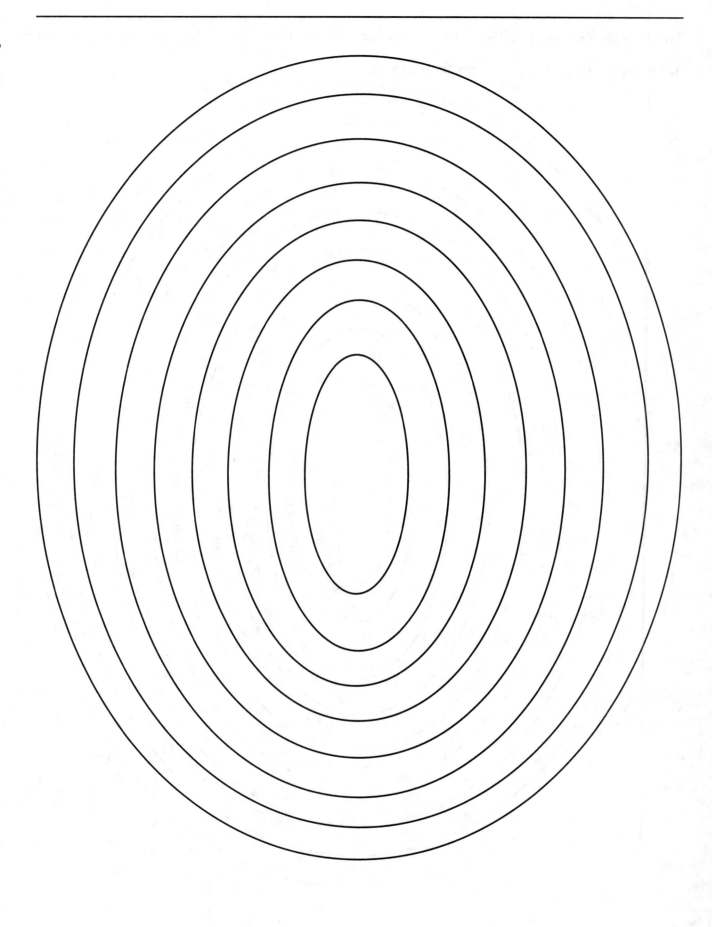

sustainability

If you take this action, will it lead toward or away from the future resource base described in your holisticgoal?

This test is perhaps the most simple and demonstrates how powerful the holisticgoal can be in decision-making. The sustainability test forces you to look at the long-term and can often provide immediate clarification about whether your decision is taking you in the direction you want to go.

Help with Testing Decisions

* Be sure you test only one decision at a time and take the simplest decisions first.

* If you can't answer a testing question quickly, drop it and go to the next one.

* An argument among decision makers often means you don't have enough basic information to answer the question.

* Don't worry too much about the Cause and Effect test if your decision is not about solving a problem.

If a decision fails a number of important tests, look for ways to modify the decision before rejecting it totally. Frequently there are compelling reasons to go ahead with a decision, and foreknowledge of weaknesses can often point the way to changes that will allow it to pass the testing next time.

Sam Bingham

Holistic Management® Certified Educator, Denver, Colorado

Raising a Child

To me, the main responsibility in raising a child is to help him or her be able to function well as an adult in our world. Most parents make most of the decisions for a child so when that child turns 18 he has had little experience in making decisions. I think children need more opportunity to make decisions or be guided in that process.

When we first started practicing Holistic Management, the kids used to tease us about testing our decisions. But especially now that they are older and having to make bigger decisions, they actually come to us to discuss how these decisions might be tested. Whether the decision is to participate as a foreign exchange student for a year, to start or end a relationship, or to stop an activity like dancing or swimming, they want to take the time to make a good decision. Testing helps them make good decisions, even if they only ask the question, "Is this action going to lead me toward what it is that I want to create?"

Robert Pasztor

High School Teacher, Albuquerque, New Mexico

weak link

The weak link test works on the principle that a chain is only as strong as its weakest link. If you spend time and energy trying to strengthen a chain by working on any link other than the weakest link, your chain will still be just as weak as it was before. In other words, you can waste a lot of time and money if you don't consider what you really need to strengthen and put your efforts there first.

The weak link test applies in three different ways: social, financial, and biological.

Social weak link

Have you considered and/or addressed any confusion, anger, or opposition this action could create with people whose support you need in the near or distant future?

In the social weak link test you consider whether the action you are contemplating, due to the prevailing attitudes and beliefs of the people affected by it, will block progress toward your holisticgoal. In other words, think about whether this is the best time to take the action or if you might actually be creating or supporting a pattern that detrimentally affects what you say you want to create.

For example, if you have a great idea that you want to implement at work, then when you run that idea through this testing question you might discover that you need to do some other things first, like taking the time to explain your idea to your coworkers or soliciting their input. Likewise, if you decide you need to discuss a concern with your significant other, if you run this decision through this testing question, you might realize that maybe the best time to discuss the concern isn't when you both feel exhausted. In both cases, the original idea might be great and move you toward your holisticgoal, but only if it passes this test. If it doesn't pass, then you are more likely to cause harm than good.

Biological weak link

In taking this action, are you addressing the weakest point in the life cycle of this organism?

In the biological weak link test you consider taking action toward organisms that you perceive as a problem because they are too few or too many in number. All organisms are most vulnerable at a certain point in their life cycle. If you know when that point is, then you can more effectively address the situation at hand.

For example, let's say you decide to plant a garden, but you have an infestation of a certain weed or bug. After researching the matter, you decide that you want to use a herbicide or insecticide. When you run that decision through this test, you need to know where the weakest point of this organism's lifecycle is. If the pesticide you have chosen affects the organism at any other time than the weakest point in its life cycle, your efforts will not be as successful as they could be, and may even fail entirely.

exercise 6-2.
weak link

purpose:
practice knowing that everything has a weak spot.

A martial arts exercise involving a wrist grab effectively demonstrates the concept of the weak link. Martial arts is based on the premise that if you understand how the body works then you are better able to defend yourself. When an assailant larger than you grabs your wrist, you have to know where the weakest part of the grip is in order to free yourself. You also have to know that no matter how strong something or someone is, we all have a vulnerable spot. (You can also read your children the Greek myth of Achilles as another example of a person's weak spot and the meaning of the phrase "Achilles' heel").

Look at the drawing below (A). Notice that the weakest part of the grip is the "opening" between where the thumb meets the fingers. It doesn't matter how strong someone is; structurally that spot is the weak link. With a very strong assailant, you might need to cause a distraction to begin this move, but once you have begun moving toward that identified weak spot (and you follow through with your move) you will break the grip.

1) Now, face your partner as in drawing (A). Have one person take the assailant role and use her right hand to grab the other person's left hand.

2) Then, as in drawing (B) and (C), the person being grabbed will rotate his left hand in a tight circle (counter clockwise) around the assailant's hand.

3) In drawing (D), the assailant must let go of the other person's hand because the move creates such stress on the thumb joint.

Sometimes this move doesn't work because people stop their circle at the least sign of resistance. In other words, they have lack of confidence in themselves and the "plan" or the move. They might also not follow the most effective "line" of movement, which is a circle. Instead, they try to yank their arm in a straight line rather than following the circle one complete rotation. Give minimal resistance at first while the defender practices the move. As she gains confidence, add more strength.

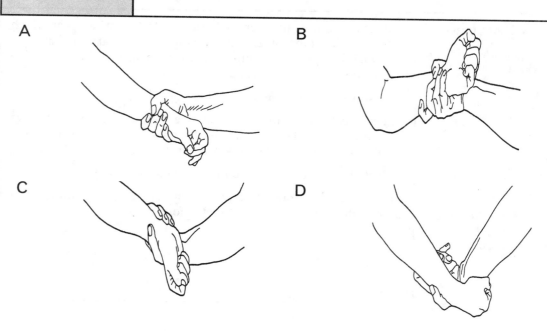

A

B

C

D

Financial weak link

Does this action strengthen the weakest link in your chain of production?

In the financial weak link, you determine where you are weakest in your ability to earn income. This test is discussed in greater detail in the financial planning chapter, Chapter Eight.

marginal reaction

Which action provides the greatest return, in terms of your holisticgoal, for the time and/or money you invest?

With the marginal reaction test you determine what is the best use of your time or money. In other words, marginal reaction is really about efficiency within the context of your holisticgoal. This test helps to ensure that, given a choice between two or more alternatives, you choose the one that moves you the most quickly toward your holisticgoal.

Another way to look at marginal reaction is the 80/20 rule. The name for that rule stems from the idea that 20 percent of what you do, leads to 80 percent of the results you get. The flip side is that the other 80 percent of what you do only leads to 20 percent of the results. So if you can discern what activities you can do with 20 percent of your time or money to yield an 80 percent return, you will make better use of your time and money. Often, if you spend small amounts of time on the planning or structuring of an activity, event, or organization, before you do all the legwork of actually putting the plan into action, you will have far more success in the implementation of your plan. By creating a structure where each action builds off of another, you will create exponential returns (like compound interest) or a resource that can regenerate rather than needing continual input or energy. The 80/20 rule is also like the law of diminishing returns; at some point the effort or money you put into something will no longer yield the return it did at the beginning.

exercise 6-3. marginal reaction	This exercise uses the marginal reaction test to make clear which action would be the better choice among the ones you are considering. The facing page has examples and blanks that you can practice with, using the directions below.
	1) List two choices you are considering.
	2) On a scale of -10 to +10, categorize how each action will move you toward your holisticgoal (+10) or away from (-10) or really won't affect your progress one way or the other (0).
purpose: practice determining marginal reaction	3) Note which one moves you forward the most and circle it.
	4) If you can't rate one or more of your choices, write down a list of the information you need to rate those choices.

exercise 6-3 (continued)	
marginal reaction	

Choice #1:   Surfing the TV
Effect on holisticgoal: -5
Choice #2:   Doing projects with the kids
Effect on holisticgoal: +5
Additional Information needed: none

---

purpose:

practice determining marginal reaction

Choice #1:   Playing soccer
Effect on holisticgoal: 7
Choice #2:   Playing hand-held video game
Effect on holisticgoal   :   0
Additional Information needed: none

Choice #1:   Going to college
Effect on holisticgoal: Not sure
Choice #2:   Dropping out
Effect on holisticgoal   :   Not sure
Additional Information needed:

How long do I have to complete the degree?

Are there other ways of getting those skills?

How much time do I have to spend on classes?

What else would I do with the time I spend studying now?

NOW IT'S YOUR TURN:

Choice #1:

Effect on holisticgoal:

Choice #2:

Effect on holisticgoal:

Additional Information needed:

A 'Holistic' House Tour

Recently I went on a "holistic" house tour. I went through my entire house—room by room, cabinet to closet to pantry, to bathrooms, basement and garage—and started questioning everything I own or buy, and its impact on my simple description of a Future Resource Base. I carried my Holistic Management framework card and my holisticgoal with me, and did my best to test each item right there on the spot.

I had hesitated to take this house tour (put it off for over a year) for fear that I'd either end up in total despair over the ecological realities of my all-too-American lifestyle, or I'd become a "green" fanatic—something I never wanted to become because I do enjoy some of my "comforts." But the deeper I got involved in holistic decision-making, the less I was able to ignore the effects of my consumer buying habits each time I turned on a light switch, flipped open a soda can, did the laundry or filled up my car with gasoline. So I decided to take Holistic Management one step deeper in my life and make the tour.

Right away, however, it became clear that I would need to do further research because in looking at all the stuff in my home, I often didn't know where it really came from or how it was manufactured—or what the true consequence of its production, packaging and shipping were to the environment. Furthermore, I often didn't know what ecologically friendly alternatives were available.

In trying to research these things, I discovered some complications—there are several competing schools of ecological thought out there today, based both on people's individual sensitivities and values, and on conflicting scientific research reports (love those paradigms!). Some folks believe there's nothing worse than petroleum-based products (including plastics) and that everything we buy should be "natural." Others feel that it is our natural resources that are in jeopardy and we shouldn't use virgin products. There are dilemmas everywhere. Should you buy a "cleaner" product that has to be flown or trucked across country using petrol and creating pollution? Or should you use a locally manufactured product that isn't as ecologically sound but doesn't have to packaged and shipped? Which are better—cloth or disposable diapers? Plastic or paper grocery bags? Paper or electronic mail? Cotton denim or polyester pants? Leather or synthetic shoes? Add to this the social ramification of how a product is made, and finally the economic realities, and it's easy to become overwhelmed.

So how do you decide what's holistically sound for your home?

Fortunately, Holistic Management is based on your own personal values—as described in your holisticgoal. And though I haven't entirely sorted out my own particular ecological/social/economic bent yet, I am at least starting to ask the right questions—before I buy.

(continued)

Throughout my house tour, I had to resist the powerful temptation to just shut down—pull that warm blanket of denial back over my head and attempt to live in ignorance once again. But of course this isn't possible—once you have truly opened your eyes, there's no going back to sleep. So I made a decision—to make one change each week. That's 52 changes in one year—not an insignificant amount. We've made a game of it at my house, researching and debating regularly at the dinner table or in the car, which changes to make this week—which has helped make something daunting into something do-able, something fun, something in keeping with my family's quality of life.

And the surprise bonus that resulted from this whole experience has been the number of people in my life whom I have personally influenced with my newly gained awareness, which just goes to show that one person really can make a difference.

Sandy Halpin

Editor of an insurance industry trade journal
Alexandria, Virginia

energy/money, source and use

Is the money or energy used in this action derived from the most appropriate source in terms of your holisticgoal? Will the way in which it is used lead you toward your holisticgoal?

This test links money and energy together because people often don't consider where or how they get these resources or their usage patterns. For example, many people do not consider fully what baggage comes along with the use of these resources (such as compound interest in the case of money or pollution in the case of energy). Yet these consequences inhibit their progress toward their holisticgoal. Likewise, how they use those resources can also hinder their progress because they don't consider if their use of this money or energy will be addictive or consumptive or just a one time consideration.

Think about whether the energy or money used in this action will move you toward your holisticgoal. For example, if you get your electricity from a utilities company that burns fossil fuel (such as coal or gas) to generate the electricity you use, then your electric use is certainly consumptive and possibly addictive depending on how you use the electricity. However, if you purchase a photovoltaic system, then you have a regenerative capacity from that one time purchase. For an additional exercise to help distinguish your natural resource use, see the Natural Resource Inventory (a6-2) in Appendix 1.

When we did the following Resource Analysis exercise as a family, we had some interesting discussions. My son, Ben, had been making a list of all the things he wanted for Christmas or his birthday (he keeps a running list). Two of the hotter items that came up were a pool table and a video game. After thinking about which category these items fell into, he realized that the pool table was in the generative category and the video game was in the degenerative category because it required a constant input of energy, and with a number of electronic or moving parts it would not last the same amount of time as a pool table. From this simple exercise he saw more clearly how the pool table was a much sounder investment (present) than the video game.

That initial reflection prompted further thought. He then wondered if he should get a foosball game (a game table with soccer players on rods with whom you hit a ball back and forth) or a pool table. Upon further reflection he realized that he could play pool by himself but not foosball so the pool table would keep him occupied more. I'm not sure he would have thought about the one question without thinking of the other.

society and culture

You need to end the testing with this question because it rounds out the picture. All of the other tests ask what you think, but this one asks how you feel. This test relies on intuition and empathy, more of the feeling and gut responses that we all use to make decisions. In this case, you consider how you feel about this decision after running it through all the testing questions and how you think it could affect others.

- How do you feel about this action now?
- Will it lead to the quality of life you desire?
- Will it adversely affect the quality of life of others?

For example, if you are considering a decision that passes every test, but you don't feel good about that decision, then don't do it until you figure out what's still bothering you. When a decision doesn't pass the society and culture test, but does pass all the other tests, then you know you need to adjust your action or plan until it does pass that test. So if you have a job opportunity that offers you meaningful work and good money, but maybe the hours don't feel right or you don't think that you will be happy there, then you need to address those factors first to make a sound decision.

Tom Frantzen and his family developed the "Testing Record" form, shown on the pages following exercise 6-4, to help them test the decisions they make on their family farm in New Hampton, Iowa. When first learning how to test decisions, some people find a more formal approach helpful. It also gives you a written record of the decisions you made and your thought process behind it, so you have a history and feedback on where you can increase your management skills. As you become more familiar with the testing process, running a decision through the testing questions happens very quickly, and often less formally.

conclusion

With these six testing questions, you now have the ability to make sound long-term decisions toward your holisticgoal. Many people practicing Holistic Management have found that running their decisions through the testing questions makes the holisticgoal more real to them. If you want to create the life you have described, these testing questions are the surest way of getting there. And as you practice this new skill you will find it gets easier and feels more natural with each decision.

exercise 6-4.
resource analysis exercise

purpose:
reflect on time, energy, and money investments

This exercise requires people to reflect on how they invest their time and money and the various connections these investments have to other parts of their lives and to the world. It also helps bring home the idea of the energy/money source and use test.

An investment is any outlay of time, money, energy, or labor. Buying a shovel, planting a tree, driving the car, taking a bath, and spending time with family are all investments in this sense. However, in order to decide the value or quality of the investment, you need to know if it is something that will continue to feed itself or need continual input. The three categories of investment are: regenerative, generative, and degenerative.

A degenerative investment is any investment that begins to fall apart as soon as the investment is made and requires on-going investment (usually an inordinate amount) to stay functional, like an automobile or an unhealthy relationship. A generative investment requires some energy in the initial investment, but saves more energy over its life than it took to create (like a well-built shovel) or provides you with a positive return (like buying an educational book). A regenerative investment can create more investment or resource from the initial outlay such as a well-designed perennial garden, a sound financial investment, or a nurturing family environment.

1) So with these categories in mind, take a piece of paper and divide it into three columns, with the headings regenerative, generative, and degenerative (you can have younger kids use "+" "0" and "-" for their headings as long as they understand the idea).

2) Take 15 minutes and evaluate your life based on these criteria.

● How do you invest your time, energy, and money?

● How about your time on the computer, for example? Watching television? Talking with your children? Spending time with extended family and friends?

● Is your energy use something that regenerates or is consumptive? What about your use of other natural resources?

● How much of the money you spend comes with no strings attached? What is the return you get from it?

Look for broad strokes and don't get bogged down in detail. Some items might land in two categories depending on your interpretation. Jot down a note next to these to help you explain your thought process later.

3) Once you've completed this part of the exercise, take a moment to look at what you wrote. How did things fall out? Where is most of your time and money invested? What's your ratio for regenerative/generative/degenerative? Are there types of investment that don't fall into just one of the categories? How about the way the investment is used? (The car, TV, computer, energy source, or loan). Once you begin to think more consciously about your choice of investment, you will begin to choose ones that help you create the life you want. Consequently, you'll have a better return from them.

Christopher Peck, a long-time teacher for Permaculture Drylands Institute and a Holistic Management® Educator, developed and uses this exercise in his workshops.

Testing Record

	Pass	Fail

Proposed Action:_____

Problem (if dealing with a problem): _____

Alternatives being compared: 1.   **2.**   **3.** _____

Cause and Effect: Does this action address the root cause of the problem?

Weak Link

    Social: Have you considered and/or addressed any confusion, anger, or opposition this action could create with people whose support you need in the near or distant future?

    Biological: (problem organism)

        Does this action address the weakest point in the life cycle of this organism?

        Are we dealing with too many or too few organisms?

        What is the weakest point in its life cycle?

        Does this action deal with it at this point?

    Financial: Does this action strengthen the weakest link in the chain of production?

Marginal Reaction (Comparing two or more actions):

    Which action provides the greatest return, in terms of your holisticgoal, for the time and money spent when compared to the alternatives?

    1. _____ 2. _____ 3. _____

    Estimate of dollars spent:_____

    Estimate hours of labor:_____

Gross Profit Analysis (Comparing two or more enterprises):

    Which enterprises contribute the most to covering the overheads of the business?

Energy/Money, Source & Use:

    ● Is the energy or money to be used derived from the most appropriate source in terms of your holisticgoal?

    ● Will the way in which the energy or money is to be used lead toward your holisticgoal?

Input testing for:	Energy	Money
Source of input		
Is it consumptive?		
Does it create dependency?		

Sustainability:

    If you take this action, will it lead toward or away from your future resource base?

Society & Culture:

    How do you feel about this action now?

    ● Will it lead to the quality of life you desire?

    ● Will it adversely affect the lives of others?

Result of this testing:

Monitoring*:

If this possible action passes, assume it's wrong if it affects the environment.

How will we know if it is a mistake (early warning criteria)?

1._____

2._____

3._____

* Monitoring is covered in Chapter Seven.

Testing a Gift Horse

Last year my mother offered to give us a horse. My parents have a horse ranch in Colorado and my mother thought a horse would be great for the kids (and of course my daughter loves horses). All we had to pay was the cost to bring the horse to our farm in Vermont. So I immediately started pricing transportation, which was turning out to be expensive. But we kept thinking, "This horse is a gift—we won't be buying the horse, just paying for the shipping—so shouldn't we do this?"

My husband and I both have jobs off the farm, so we do have some discretionary income for things that in the past have fallen under the category of "general desires" for the family. But something was nagging at the back of our minds about this decision.

Finally, I was a phone call away from hiring the shippers, when my husband Phil said, "Let's just run it through the testing." So we did. We tested taking the horse against not taking it. Well, the gift horse started failing all the tests, particularly the financial ones. This horse wasn't going to earn us any income on the farm; it would require feed and possibly new fencing and even a shelter. And we know almost nothing about taking care of horses.

But even more powerful than the financial tests was the realization that this horse failed our holisticgoal. We want to have a close, caring family where we do things together as a family. With one horse and four people, we wouldn't be able to enjoy the horse as a family—maybe at most, two people would enjoy the horse together (one riding and one leading) but for the most part, the horse would be yet another solitary pursuit for one of us. Our real wealth as a family is time, and this horse was going to take time (and resources) away from us, rather than bring us together.

So now we had to figure out how to give the horse back to my mother. We thought about our holisticgoal which includes strengthening our extended family, and it dawned on us that for the price of shipping the horse out here, we could instead afford to fly the whole family out to my parents' ranch for a week, and spend time with them! They have lots of horses there, and all the equipment and expertise, and we could spend a week riding horses together, which would probably be more than we'd be able to do with the one horse at home. So our decision was obvious at that point.

What amazes me about the testing is that once you do it, you see the right decision so clearly, you can't talk yourself out of it. For the first time, I was really able to see how to put my money toward my true values. Prior to this, we sort of went along thinking, "well it sounds like a good idea and we have the money to do it, so why not?" But the testing has given us a way to see clearly where our money's going and what's really important to us.

Chris Knippenberg

Occupational Therapist and Part-Time Livestock Producer
Hartland, Vermont
Excerpted from Holistic Management: A New Framework for Decision-Making by Allan Savory with Jody Butterfield.

7

charting and staying on course

planning and monitoring

key concepts in
this chapter

planning:
charting
your course

monitoring:
keeping on track

Now that you've learned how to use the testing questions with your day to day decisions, the next step is to learn how Holistic Management incorporates planning and monitoring. Because plans require many decisions before we even act, using a planning process that continually refers to your holisticgoal helps to create a sound plan to which everyone is committed. While many people create inspiring plans, few can actually carry them to fruition if they require work or support from other people who aren't committed to that plan.

Because your planning is an extension of your holisticgoal, you should have all the key players invested in the plan. This investment is even more crucial in the monitoring stage of any plan because it is a rare plan indeed that works just as it was planned. Far too many plans have fallen by the wayside because of poor monitoring, or response to critical information, than because of lack of forethought in the planning process. Therefore, the commitment to seeing a plan to completion through monitoring and readjusting of that plan is an even more critical component to the planning process.

To put this in the context of our sailing metaphor, a captain and crew must make plans for any long voyage. They must decide where they want to sail, what route they will take, what cargo they will carry, or what time of year they will travel. They might even start planning their return voyage. If they have even greater aspirations such as building a successful shipping company, discovering new lands, or helping people travel to new lands and opportunity, they will need to consider many more factors before they even set sail.

So having a clear sense of where you are headed lays the groundwork for a successful voyage. By charting the best course, you will know when you are on or off course with greater accuracy so you will be able to adapt more readily to any change in your plan. But if you forge ahead with the plans you made based on what you wanted to hear rather than careful research, or if you choose not to monitor your progress as you face the many challenges life offers, your chance of getting shipwrecked or stuck in the doldrums will increase.

> ### Family Planning
>
> I started involving the children in mainly materialistic planning. Meg (13), for instance, just simply had to have a CD player, and not any old one either. So I started her on an allowance system this year and we worked out what she needed to save if she wanted to achieve her goal by November.
>
> We often discuss what the children might like to do after school and how we as a family can all help each other achieve those plans. This kind of planning has affected us in other ways. For example, I had packed the TV away and expected the children to pressure me to replace it. But after the holidays, they remarked on how much nicer it was without the TV as we would all sit and chat or read in the evening instead of watching the biggest load of rubbish on TV just because it was there.
>
> But the biggest change has come about in our discussions—they are far more constructive and seem to have lost the confrontational element to a large extent because they are more goal-oriented. As a result of thorough and systematic planning, I'm finding that I can spend more time with the children. It has also improved my productivity because it made me realize I was spending more time stamping out fires than actually getting down to the more important issues and work.
>
> Linda Walker
>
> Rancher
> Graaff-Reinet, South Africa

planning: charting your course

Planning is your commitment to the long-term decisions you make. If you make a decision that you've put a great deal of thought into (like refinancing a mortgage, building a house, or obtaining more training), then you need to determine the steps it will take to put that decision into action. In other words, planning is a series of decisions that you make about your future that may or may not come to fruition depending on your planning, monitoring (observing and analyzing feedback), and ability to respond to that monitoring and to life. In this way, monitoring, analysis of feedback, and response to that feedback is a critical part of planning.

The tricky part of planning for some people is that they believe they never plan, so the concept seems foreign to them. But, we often do use elements of planning subconsciously. If you make a grocery list, carpool the kids, or take a vacation, you have planned. Obviously, there are different levels of complexity in planning, but how you prepare will greatly impact the results you get in carrying out those activities.

Some people think that planning is an attempt to control the future. But planning is preparing for the future, laying the groundwork to help create the best possible outcome.

The best possible outcome may not always happen, but you will have done your best and probably helped to create the second best possible outcome in the process.

Planning can be scary because it's a big commitment. Instead of hoping something will happen you are saying, "I'm going to help make this happen." That kind of attitude can generate and attract a lot of enthusiasm and excitement, which helps motivate people when it comes time to do the nitty-gritty work of putting the plan into action.

The good news is that you've already taken the first step in good planning; you have a clear sense of where you want to go because you have a holisticgoal. With your holisticgoal and the testing questions, you have tools to assure that you are more likely to stay on track.

The keys to good planning are:

- Being clear about what you want to create
- Assessing resources and liabilities
- Knowing as many of the factors as possible that will affect the plan
- Considering as many alternatives as possible
- Sifting through all the possibilities
- Choosing the one that looks best in the context of a larger picture

You can use these keys for any kind of planning and the Holistic Financial Planning process does.

The good thing about creating a plan is that you can think of all the factors ahead of time so you don't have to do that sort of creative thinking when you might have a number of other things to consider. If you think of as many things as possible ahead of time, you are more likely to succeed or cope with changes or unexpected events as they arise.

Thousands of people have talent. I might as well congratulate you for having eyes in your head. The one and only thing that counts is: Do you have staying power?

—Noel Coward

| exercise 7-1. planning exercise | 1) Have everyone in your group select an activity they like to do (play video games, play sports, sew, hunt, cook, garden, etc.).
2) Have each person break down the steps (necessary planning) to engage in the activity. These steps should include everything from the pre-activity (getting to the event) to the post-activity (clean up). You might need to circulate the lists to see if people listed thoroughly all the necessary steps. See the sample list on the next page.
3) Next, everyone should list the necessary skills for that activity. Look at the sample list on the next page to get an idea of what skills you might include.
4) Then have each person make a plan for something she wants to achieve (learn a new skill, acquire a new possession, etc.) Have each person use the plan s/he created as a template or as a model for what s/he wants to do. As a group, you can also help each person identify resources and limitations, factors that may influence his/her plan, and alternatives to his/her plans.
5) Test all options toward either an individual's or the family's holisticgoal. |
| **purpose:** recognize skills we already have, how they might be of use in the future, and how to plan new activities | |

Planning Exercise

Current activity: Woodworking

Planning steps:

1. Pick design
2. Pick wood
3. Calculate supplies
4. Purchase supplies
5. Organize shop
6. Organize supplies
7. Measure wood
8. Cut wood
9. Fasten pieces
10. Sand
11. Finish
12. Clean up

Skills needed:

1. Math for calculations
2. Precision for measuring
3. Decision-making for wood choice and design
4. Eye/hand coordination for operating equipment
5. Spatial ability for putting together
6. Persistence to get the job done
7. Creativity in design

New activity: Buy pool table

Planning steps:

1. Research cost
2. Research where to buy
3. Research brands
4. Start savings account for money
5. Put aside 50% of gift money
6. Make money with additional chores
7. Start lawn service business

Skills needed:

1. Math
2. Persistence to put money in savings instead of spending
3. Creativity to think of other chores or use of time
4. Sales ability to get business

Resources and factors:

1. Gift money
2. Work at home
3. Parents help with research
4. Newspaper—Classifieds
5. Library—Consumer Reports
6. Do more work in winter when I don't have soccer
7. Do more work on Sundays when I don't have soccer
8. Get friends involved

Planning Exercise

Current activity

Planning steps:

1. _____
2. _____
3. _____
4. _____
5. _____
6. _____
7. _____
8. _____
9. _____
10. _____
11. _____
12. _____

Skills needed:

1. _____
2. _____
3. _____
4. _____
5. _____
6. _____

New activity

Planning steps:

1. _____
2. _____
3. _____
4. _____
5. _____
6. _____
7. _____

Skills needed:

1. _____
2. _____
3. _____
4. _____
5. _____
6. _____

Resources and factors:

1. _____
2. _____
3. _____
4. _____
5. _____
6. _____
7. _____
8. _____

monitoring: keeping on track

If you want to make a plan succeed, you must have a clear sense of how to monitor the results so you are better able to see unintended consequences at the earliest possible moment. Moreover, you must analyze that information and determine the best way to change or adjust your plan in the context of that information. While many people monitor, they don't notice the signs until they are already severely off track (their spouse wants a divorce, their kids ignore them, they are already in debt).

Good monitoring means catching yourself going off track just as it begins to happen. Of course, this ability is the ideal. But think about when you first learned a new skill like riding a bike; you were probably all over the road because you didn't know how to distribute your weight properly or how to point the front tire in the direction you wanted to go. In essence, you couldn't monitor effectively because you didn't have the skill. You knew you were off track when you veered off the road or the bike tilted to the point that you almost fell over. But that level of response is not the same as sensing the slight movement of the bike to one side or the other almost as it happens so that you never even wobble. As you ride a bike you constantly adjust your weight as the surface changes or as you need to change direction. You become skilled at responding to those factors. That kind of response is an example of effective monitoring.

Monitoring really requires three skills: knowing what kind of outcome you want, observation, and analysis of the observation. One game that helps to increase monitoring skills (observation and analysis) is charades. In charades you have to observe people's actions to make sense of what they are trying to communicate. But, people have problems with charades because they get stuck interpreting a clue in one way. Once they focus on that interpretation they either don't notice other cues the "actor" offers or they interpret those cues based on the picture they have already created in their mind.

exercise 7-2. observation skills **purpose:** improve your ability to observe	Take an 8 1/2" by 11" square of cardboard. Cut out the inner part so you have a frame that is about 1" wide all the way around. Have each member of your family take a turn at placing that frame on the ground outside your home. How many things can they observe within that square? See if you can beat your personal best in another location. For a real challenge, you can toss it and see where it lands. You'll notice that your ability to discern small details will increase rapidly because you are intent on noticing as many distinctions as possible.

When monitoring plans in day-to-day life, you have to determine what clues will help you know when your plan has gone awry. Prior to implementing a plan, decide what things you can monitor to indicate whether you might be getting off track. The earliest indicators are the best. Allan Savory uses the analogy of the miners who took canaries into the mines to help them discern gas leaks. If the canary died, the miners knew they had to get out to avoid asphyxiation. So you want to figure out what indicators will tell you your plan is off at the dead canary stage, not the dead miner stage.

Again, this level of monitoring is an ideal to work towards. It's hard to do two things at once. Setting the monitoring criteria ahead of time for any decision or plan, when you can focus, helps you to think more clearly in any given moment, especially when you are in crisis. Make sure you set up times for reflection so you can look back over the week or the month and assess your progress with your various plans whether they involve social, environmental, or financial decisions.

If that kind of rigorous process sounds like a lot of work, then figure out how to make it more fun. Monitoring can seem like the hardest part of planning or the least rewarding because you can never succeed as perfectly as you would have liked. But monitoring can became an opportunity to recognize all the things you are doing well and to acknowledge those successes. In education, parenting, or relationships, you get far more results by encouraging desired behaviors than chastising people for undesired behaviors—which doesn't mean you can't offer constructive criticism. But you need to consistently monitor for the behaviors or results you want, decide what an appropriate "success" rate is, notice when those results have or haven't happened, replan to have them happen more frequently, and celebrate any success.

conclusion

Making a plan and monitoring it can take a lot of work, but it's the only way to insure that your long-term goals or objectives succeed. In planning, you can map out details that require forethought, research, and discussion. In monitoring, you can determine the way to make sure you stay on track. But with holistic planning, you also use your holisticgoal as the foundation for monitoring and replanning. That way, your planning moves you toward what you want rather than to solve problems.

Do not weep; do not wax indignant. Understand.

—Baruch Spinoza

exercise 7-3.
developing monitoring criteria

purpose:

practice in monitoring

Several of the exercises in this book ask that you have a person play the role of a monitor. This person observes the players in an exercise and analyzes what happened. The next skill to practice is developing monitoring criteria.

1) To practice developing monitoring criteria choose an action you are contemplating. In the space provided on the next page, write down the criteria.

2) In the first column, list all the outcomes that would tell you that you had made a wise decision. These are the criteria that indicate you are on the right track.

3) In the second column, list all the outcomes that would tell you that you needed to change your plan. Think about what the physical signs would indicate when you are on or off target (such as happy faces, stress, withdrawal, etc.). Look at the sample lists below to get some ideas.

For ongoing monitoring, keep these lists handy. You can rate your progress according to the criteria on the lists. If it is a new plan, you might want to check weekly to see if you are on track or need to adjust your plan. Remember, adjusting a plan is just like making one. Follow the same keys to good planning referred to earlier.

EXAMPLE:

Decision: To change schools

Criteria to show on track	Criteria to show off track
Children and parents are happy (smiling faces)	Children are uncomfortable (don't participate)
Children are learning (excited about going)	Children are bored (don't have anything to share about their day)
Children feel challenged	Children are scared (not eager to go)
Parents feel a part of the school (spend time there or work on projects for school)	Parents feel stressed meeting financial obligations (Impacting finances more than we thought)
People at the school are friendly (develop friendships)	Parents feel stressed meeting responsibilities (Adversely affecting time more than we thought)
It's easy to get to and from school (logistics aren't a problem)	Parents don't feel connected to people there (detached)
Parents contribute to the school (feel valued)	Parents can't find a way to contribute (frustrated)
	Administration doesn't respond to parents' suggestions

Decision:

Criteria to show on track	Criteria to show off track

My husband was out of work in his construction trade for a year. We were in debt and getting deeper. There didn't seem to be a way out. So I brought my farm books and financial records along to my first Holistic Financial Planning workshop. I was inspired the first day by the fact that I could have some control over my financial situation, so I went through the books that night to see where and how the money was being spent. I also looked at the enterprises individually and was very surprised at what I found. I made a vow that night to not increase the debt and to refinance the loans. Right then and there, I developed a plan to pay off the loans sooner. We have stuck very close to that plan since and are slowly reducing that debt. We were able to put some money away from every paycheck and drastically reduced (and eventually eliminated) the enterprises that were creating a loss. The farm, which traditionally lost a great deal of money, is now making some.

Sticking to a financial plan has been difficult for some members of our family. There is a great deal of "spontaneity" among family members. Old habits are hard to break. I can say, however, that we are doing better than we were before Holistic Management. I had to realize that people can't always change overnight and that learning comes in stages that cannot be rushed.

Sandy Matheson

Holistic Management® Certified Educator
Bellingham, Washington

8

outfitting your ship

financial planning

Many people get hooked on Holistic Management because of the financial planning. With finances you can see the immediate concrete results (debt decreasing, profit increasing). People who fail with other financial planning processes succeed with Holistic Managemen® Financial Planning because this planning process builds on their holisticgoal. Once people have identified what is most important to them and have committed to making it happen (ownership in their holisticgoal), they are more willing to do what it takes to make it happen—financially as well as socially and environmentally.

And just as a good business needs a financial plan that produces profit in a manner that is socially and environmentally sustainable, a family can also benefit from such a plan as they move toward what they have identified as the life they want.

the importance of profit

Profit is simply income minus expenses. If you earn a high income and spend all of it, you have no profit. If you want to have choices and to be able to explore opportunities, you need to create profit. The first part of profit is income. Many families have the salaries that their income producers bring home. Others, who are self-employed, have whatever income they can generate from their business. Some people are salaried employees and derive additional income from a home business or enterprise as well. In some families, children are involved in family enterprises or businesses, or have their own enterprises (the proverbial lemonade stand). There are infinite ways of earning money and this planning process will help you to determine if you want to engage in additional or different enterprises in line with your holisticgoal. Those people who are interested in only earning money from their salaries can skip any of the steps in the Holistic Management® Financial Planning process that relate to decisions about enterprises.

One of the best ways to determine your ability to create profit is to take a large piece of graph paper and plot out your income starting from the day you received your first paycheck. Now total the income from all those years. It might surprise you how much you've earned. Next, estimate how much your expenses were the first year you were responsible for paying your own bills. If you can't remember exactly, but know you didn't go in debt that first year, you can assume that your expense total was the same as your income that year. So take that total and multiply it by the number of years you've been working. If you want to be more accurate, you can add inflation to your expense figures. Subtract that total from your income total. That is an example of all the profit you could have produced to date if your expenses had stayed the same.

Many people let their expenses rise to match the level of the income they expect to receive. So even though they may have earned $500,000 over the course of 20 years, they may have spent all of that or more. If they had kept their expenses from rising as their income rose, they could have saved or invested hundreds of thousands of dollars. Which brings us to the second part of creating profit: controlling expenses. Again the holisticgoal helps you determine how your spending can help you create the life you want rather than the life you think you should live. So the way you produce profit and invest it will take into account that which you value and need.

principles of holistic management® financial planning

- You have a clear sense of what you want to create (your holisticgoal)
- You know how to test your decisions (financial and otherwise) toward your holisticgoal
- You understand the importance of planning and monitoring
- You recognize the psychological importance of planning profit before you plan expenses

the planning process

Think about your planning session as the time to decide on your family's yearly focus. This can be a time of great excitement and anticipation as everyone contributes to the discussion. You'll have to decide how to best adapt the process to your family's unique needs, situation, and timetable. Some families choose to take a long weekend in a retreat-type setting to complete the whole process at one time while others prefer to make each piece of the process a separate session. Then they set a series of meetings to make sure they complete these sessions so they can create their plan in a timely fashion.

But having fun and encouraging creativity is just as important in this planning process. Many good ideas come from lively brainstorming sessions. Moreover, many people rank financial planning right up there with going to the dentist, so you need to make it fun if you want everyone involved, not just the wannabe bean counters. Because some people have such a big block on financial planning, make sure everything is on paper, so everyone can follow along. If any idea is abstract, make it as concrete as possible, especially when you involve children. You can even use play money to help them calculate income and expenses. Some adults might also appreciate such an exercise.

Income & Expense Tracking

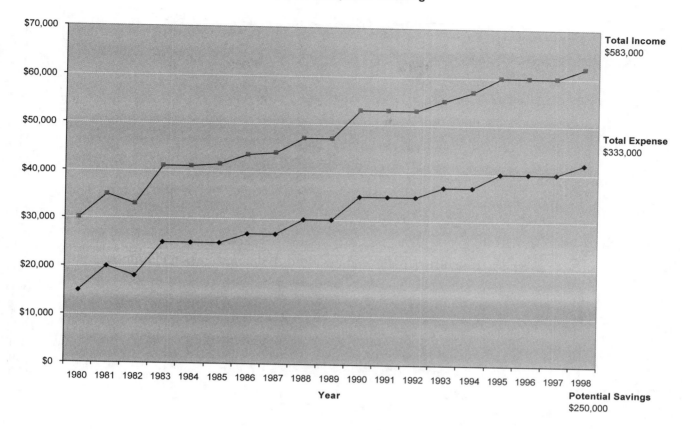

There are sample worksheets in Appendix 4 to help you generate ideas on how you can use the forms that the Holistic Management International created for this process. These include:

Worksheets: Easy to use, simple grid sheets that replace all scrap paper. Once you calculate your figures on these sheets for various enterprises or expenses, you can use that information for planning many times throughout the year.

Annual Income and Expense Plan spreadsheets: A large spreadsheet for the year that includes space for not only your planned and actual figures, but also space for recording the difference between those two figures for the month and cumulatively month after month. (These latter figures help you monitor and control your plan). When you create this plan, you transfer all the totals from the worksheets on to this spreadsheet so you can see the big financial picture and make adjustments.

Control Sheets: Sheets used in the monitoring phase to record variations in planned and actual figures. These sheets also have spaces for recording the actions that will bring your plan back in line as well as the person/people responsible for completing those actions.

Holistic Management International offers a comprehensive guide to Holistic Management® Financial Planning and has developed financial planning software. Because this planning process encourages a great deal of creativity and exploration, the software helps you experiment all you want without the tedious re-calculation of figures that slows many people down.

Financial Planning for the Future

Setting our holisticgoal has been a great savings for us. We now spend only in a direction that will lead us to our holisticgoal and the quality of life described in it. In the past, we spent haphazardly as we tried to alleviate an immediate crisis, thus treating a symptom rather than the cause. When a problem came up, we found a shortcut to solve it, with little regard to the bigger picture or any long term planning. When we planned like that, we found that a few years down the road our quick fix became redundant as our plans and ideas had changed.

Philip and Lindsay Theron

Ranchers
Venterstad, South Africa

So to start using the Holistic Management® Financial Planning process you will need 15-20 worksheets, and at least one annual spreadsheet, or the computer software. When you begin the planning process you will want a worksheet on hand. As you do your research you'll make calculations that you need to record on worksheets so you have the supporting information on hand when you begin to make comparisons and decisions. When you actually begin the planning phase you have only to transfer the totalled figures from your worksheets to the spreadsheet. As you begin monitoring your plan, you will record the totals that you actually earn or spend in the "actuals" rows on the spreadsheet. Next, you calculate the differences for the month or cumulatively to date before transferring those figures to your monthly control sheets to determine how to keep on plan.

This process is far more comprehensive than merely preparing an annual budget. It continually asks you to question previous assumptions and to look at new possibilities. In preparing a budget, you take predetermined income and expense figures and juggle them until they balance. Your choices often are just a matter of eliminating expenses. Moreover, when people prepare their household budgets, they rarely ask the question of how to increase income in order to increase profit (i.e. investments, savings, or reinvesting into the family business). This question can be just as important for a family in which the income earners are salaried as it is for a family running a home business.

With this planning process, you are consistently and rigorously looking at what you are doing and why. In this way you can become far more creative about how much income you want to earn, how much profit you want, and how you might more effectively control expenses so you can earn that profit.

phase I: preliminary planning sessions

As you prepare for your preliminary sessions you should consider whom you want to invite besides the income earners in the family. For example, your children can become income earners as you consider new enterprises, or as they help you in an enterprise in which you are already engaged. Certainly, they will influence your spending habits. Likewise, you can invite people you know who are open-minded or creative thinkers to help you generate new ideas or view things differently. They can be especially helpful if they are not involved in your line of work and have no preconceived notion of how things should be done.

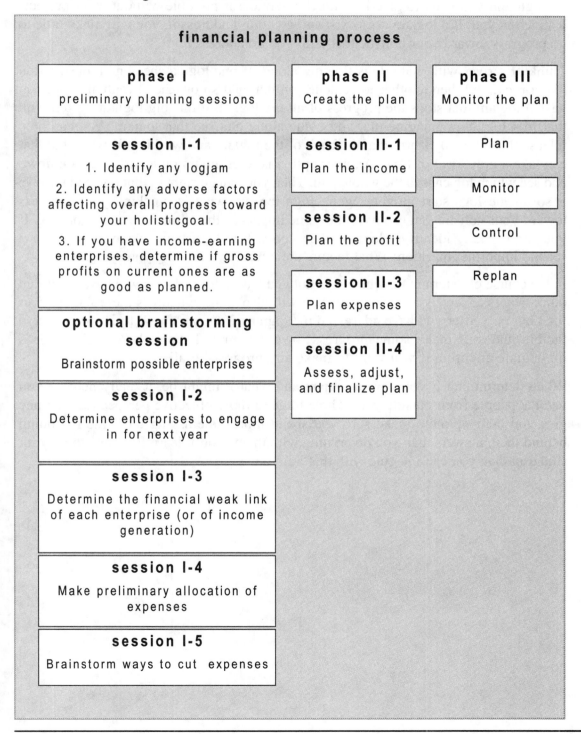

financial planning process

phase I
preliminary planning sessions

phase II
Create the plan

phase III
Monitor the plan

session I-1
1. Identify any logjam
2. Identify any adverse factors affecting overall progress toward your holisticgoal.
3. If you have income-earning enterprises, determine if gross profits on current ones are as good as planned.

optional brainstorming session
Brainstorm possible enterprises

session I-2
Determine enterprises to engage in for next year

session I-3
Determine the financial weak link of each enterprise (or of income generation)

session I-4
Make preliminary allocation of expenses

session I-5
Brainstorm ways to cut expenses

session II-1
Plan the income

session II-2
Plan the profit

session II-3
Plan expenses

session II-4
Assess, adjust, and finalize plan

Plan

Monitor

Control

Replan

session I-1: identifying a possible logjam

Once everyone has assembled, you focus on the first step: determining if there is a logjam. A logjam is anything that keeps you from making significant progress toward your holisticgoal. You may or may not have a logjam, but if you feel stuck then it is likely that you do.

The logjam question is one that you probably won't examine more than once a year. Once you identify a major block to progress, you want to give yourself the time to build momentum to move through it. Often a big logjam might take some time to work through and you want to give it as much attention as possible without other projects distracting you. If a logjam does exist and you don't address it, you will make little to no progress toward your holisticgoal until you do address it.

Think of a river with many logs floating along. If one log catches on an obstruction like a rock, and then another log catches on that and so on, then eventually you can have a logjam that stops the progress of all the logs. But this big logjam started with that first log. Now imagine that you come along and see that logjam. You can help release those logs by starting at the back of the logjam and working forward, but that can take a great deal of time. Another option is to climb up on a cliff and look down and see which log caused the whole jam. Then you can go right to that one and remove it so all the logs start moving again. Figuring out what is blocking your progress toward your holisticgoal can have the same impact in the whole you are managing. If you can't readily identify a logjam, then you will at least have begun to answer the second important question: What factors are adversely affecting your progress?

In the course of determining whether or not you have a logjam, you will have identified other factors adversely affecting you. You will also want to address these factors over time but only after you have addressed the logjam. You can chose to ignore adverse factors and still make some progress toward your holisticgoal. A logjam needs immediate attention if you want to make any progress at all.

When determining if you have a logjam and what it might be, it really helps if you involve people from outside your whole to get a more objective perspective. As they give you their opinion, make sure you spend more time asking them the reasoning behind their answers than you do arguing with them. You'll learn far more about your situation than you can imagine with that attitude.

exercise 8-1.
logjam exercise

purpose:
find the greatest adverse effect

In the example to the right, a family has decided to refinance their home. In this scenario, they wrote down all the various factors that were impeding progress toward their holisticgoal. After writing down all these factors, they arranged them to determine which ones had the greatest adverse effect. They moved those factors toward the bottom of the page until they concluded that their mortgage had the greatest impact. From that information they decided to refinance.

1) On a sheet of paper brainstorm all the concerns, needs, wants, and commitments that affect movement toward your holisticgoal.

2) Use the empty circles in the empty logjam diagram to record the results. Use a pencil because you will probably have to erase and rearrange as you decide which concerns have greater influence.

3) Begin arranging and sorting the concerns or issues to see where patterns lie and what might underlie several concerns. As you work, funnel the concerns that have the greatest adverse impact on your holisticgoal toward the bottom of the page to see if you can identify a logjam. Remember the symbol of the logjam. If you find that something is blocking your overall progress, then when you remove it, you will make greater progress toward creating the life you want.

4) Once you have identified a logjam, then you can brainstorm what you'd like to do to remove it. In the sample, the high mortgage situation made it apparent that refinancing was the best bet for the family's money. For others, the logjam might be of a social or environmental nature (such as alcoholism or owning a home built on a toxic waste dump). With this exercise you can determine one thing you want to work on and allow yourself an extended amount of time to give it adequate attention.

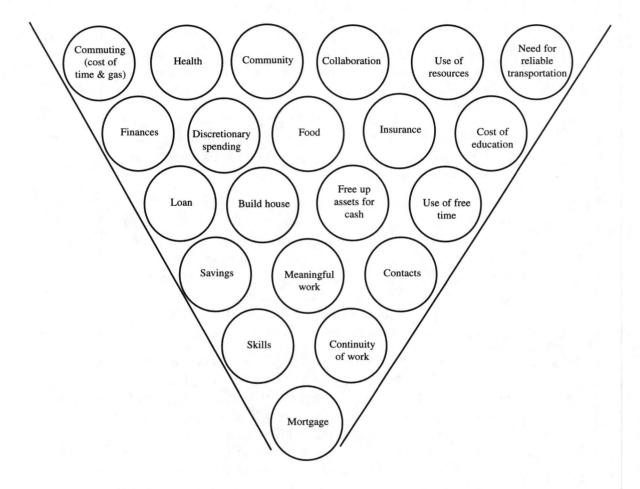

Focus:
High-interest mortgage
Decision:
Refinance

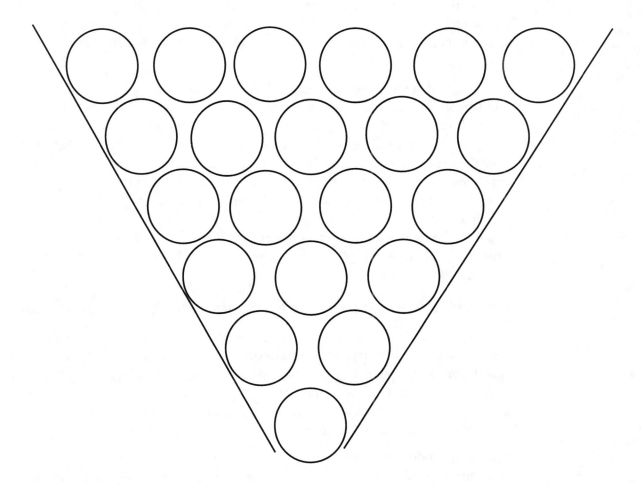

Focus:

Decision:

gross profit analysis

You use the gross profit analysis test when you choose between two or more income-generating enterprises. In this test you simply figure out all the direct costs for that enterprise and subtract them from all the direct income you would receive from that enterprise. In doing so, you determine which enterprise will give you the most gross profit. This test is simple, but very helpful as you explore alternative enterprises. Each year, before engaging in new enterprises, you need to analyze your enterprises as part of the annual review to see if your gross profit was as good as planned. In this way, you can make a better-informed decision about your current enterprises in the coming year.

For example, let's say that you've decided to do some woodworking at home for additional income. You have a number of contacts and ideas about which products you will make. To decide which enterprises would give you the best gross profit, you would calculate all the costs for material, how many of the items you could produce over the year, and the income they would produce. Then subtract from that total all the expenses you would incur to produce them. Then you do the same calculations for the other enterprise. Once you have that information, you can use the other testing questions to help complete the decision. Remember, the gross profit analysis test is only one test and must be used with the others to get the full picture of how best to proceed. For an example of a more comprehensive gross profit analysis, see the financial samples in Appendix 4.

optional session: brainstorming possible enterprises

If you do earn income from enterprises, it helps to brainstorm new enterprises periodically because people often assume they can earn income in only one way. But if you consider all your options and possibilities, you can make better decisions or feel more confident about the decisions you make. You probably won't brainstorm a new enterprise each year as new enterprises usually require more time to start than to develop already existing enterprises.

The number one rule of brainstorming is: Be creative. Try a warm-up exercise first to get everyone relaxed (something like brainstorming all the ways you can use a golf ball). Then give everyone 10 minutes to come up with all the different enterprises anyone in your family could engage in to create additional income, given your interests, talents, location, etc. Don't criticize, edit, or comment on anyone's suggestions. Try to piggyback on as many ideas as possible and have fun. See if you can generate at least 100 ideas, but don't take more than the allotted 10 minutes.

Next, narrow down your choices to the three or four most likely enterprises:

- Use the society and culture test to eliminate any enterprises that would not be in line with your values.
- Drop any ideas that are absolutely ridiculous or impossible (but be careful how quickly you determine that any of the enterprises fall into this category).
- Do a rough gross profit analysis to see how the remaining ideas contribute financially.
- Use the rest of the testing questions to see which enterprises will take you furthest toward your holisticgoal.

exercise 8-3.

gross profit analysis for enterprises

purpose:

profit analysis for enterprises find out which enterprise gives the highest gross profit

List the gross income and expenses for the three to four enterprises you selected. Rate them in order of highest gross profit.

Enterprise	Rating	Expenses			Income			Gross Profit		
		Good	Average	Poor	Good	Average	Poor	Good	Average	Poor

exercise 8-2.

brainstorm
income-
generating
ideas

purpose:

find the things
that would best
help you create
the life you
want in the
coming year

1) Use a separate sheet of paper to list all your brainstorming ideas. Use of an easel pad or a white board on a wall helps to keep all the ideas visible to everyone during the exercise.

2) Use the society and culture test to eliminate any enterprises that would not be in line with your values. Draw a line through the ones that don't pass and put a "SC" next to them to remind you which test they failed.

3) Now look at any of the ideas that are absolutely ridiculous or impossible (remember to be careful how quickly you determine if an enterprises falls into this category). Draw a line through any ideas that fail and put an "R."

3) Now do a rough gross profit analysis to see how the remaining ideas contribute financially. Put the calculated figure next to the remaining ideas.

4) Use the rest of the testing questions to see which enterprises will take you furthest toward your holisticgoal. Put "MR" next to the ones that have the highest marginal reaction for time or money expended. Put "EM" next to the ones that pass the Energy/Money, Source and Use test. Put "S" for those that move you toward the future resource base in your holisticgoal. Put "CE" next to the ideas that pass Cause and Effect. At this point you'll have a pretty good picture of which enterprises are most promising.

5) List your top three to four choices for the year.

a)

b)

d)

e)

session I-2: determining which enterprises to engage in

At this point you will do a more detailed or accurate gross profit analysis on the possible enterprises to determine which will generate the most income. Use worksheets to record all your figures. (See Appendix 4 for a sample Gross Profit Analysis.)

<u>Applying the Weak Link Test</u>

Holistic Management® Financial Planning has been particularly important to us. When we started we were on a very tight budget and did our monitoring weekly to ensure that we were on track as we were only able to plan an $800 safety margin, which is not a lot over a year. One of the main decisions we made then was not to rent a house/flat as we spend about nine to ten months a year traveling. Instead, we stayed with my twin sister whenever we were in Johannesburg. This continued for the first 18 months. We were then in a position to afford to rent a place of our own. When doing our plan for 1997, we tested the decision to rent a place. It failed the financial weak link test, but it had become a priority on the social side, so we decided it was time to get our own place.

Another major decision we faced was that within two years we had moved from a marketing weak link to a resource weak link. We needed help. Initially we were looking for someone to help us both—a trainee educator who could help Dick with the training and who could help me with the administration. On testing the decision we realized that we do not want to become a bureaucracy of educators in southern Africa. But we wanted to encourage others to become educators so that we can all work independently but in collaboration. So for the past year we have been on an active campaign to encourage others to become educators and now have three people mentoring with us until a regional educator program starts. And in the meantime, I have employed someone part-time to help with the administration. We attribute our ability to make these sound decisions within complex situations to holistic decision-making.

Judy Richardson

Whole Concepts
Vorna Valley, South Africa

session I-3: determining the financial weak link

Like the logjam test, you usually only use the financial weak link test once a year to give it adequate attention. This test helps you know where you will direct your time and money for that year so that you maximize the income you receive from any particular enterprise or income producer.

This test is based on the chain of production. Everyone engages in a chain of production whether they know it or not. There are three basic stages in that chain (resource conversion, product conversion, and marketing or money conversion). This chain is easy to see in the context of a business like a lumber company in which they must grow trees (resources), make them into lumber (product), and market them in order to turn their resources and labor into money. In the case of a business that provides a service, the resources are mainly staff and capital; the product is the service

---

exercise 8-4.
chain of
production

purpose:
find out the
weak link for
an enterprise

Variation A: Below is the outline to evaluate one enterprise. Copy the components for each enterprise you want to test. If you don't have any enterprises because you earn all your income as an employee, skip this exercise and go to the Chain of Improvement Exercise.

Using the circles below, determine the weakest link in each of your enterprises and list ways to strengthen that link.

Enterprise _____

  Resources   Product   Marketing

Weak Link_____

Ideas for strengthening the weak link

Variation B: Holistic Management® Certified Educator Mark Gardner offers another way to determine your weak link.

1) Get as many people as possible who know your situation to write down all the financial issues that face your family and/or business.

2) Explain the concept of the chain of production to them.

3) Have them list all the issues under the part of the chain of production to which they think they relate.

4) See which list is the longest. Chances are that that part of the chain of production is the weakest. You can use this same exercise for Exercise 8-5, "Chain of Improvement."

exercise 8-5. chain of improvement **purpose:** find out the financial weak link for an individual	The chain of improvement is a variation of the financial weak link test. Like the financial weak link test, this exercise helps you decide what each income producer needs to improve to generate more income (if that is necessary to achieving their holisticgoal). To do so, they must determine or develop their "product" (what they want to do and where their strengths or weaknesses lie), produce it (acquire content skills or knowledge), and engage with others to share or sell that product (communication and interpersonal expertise). In other words, in a given year, a family or individual needs to decide if the weakest link in their chain of improvement is their ability to know what they have to offer or want to contribute, their technical skills in achieving it, or their ability to engage with others. For example, a family member might not be sure what she wants to do with her life, or she may know but not have the technical skills, or she may have the technical skills, but not the social skills. If you want to be an accountant and you have the technical skills, but your social skills are lacking, then you may find it hard to get the kind of job you want until you address that issue. Remember, this is for financial planning and is used to help you decide how you can generate more income either through an existing enterprise/career or in establishing a new enterprise/career. With that in mind, look at the examples on the following page. Make a copy of the blank chain below for each income producer in the family to fill out for the jobs or enterprises with which he or she is involved. Once you have that information, you can use the other testing questions to help you decide what time, energy, or strategies you will put toward strengthening your weakest link. While you might have areas of weakness in each link of the chain, only one is the weakest. Focus on this one first until it is strengthened.

(law, therapy, management consulting, etc.); and marketing is everything involved in getting your service to your clients. If you don't know which part of that production chain is the weakest, then you might easily spend a great deal of money in one area that will not give you the same return that you could have generated by spending a smaller amount in the right place. If you keep making those same kind of decisions over time you can get yourself into some serious financial trouble.

However, by using this test, you can direct sometimes small amounts to the right area and get amazing returns. So examine your business or your ability to generate income as an employee, and see which one of those three areas is your weakest. That is your financial weak link.

Any money you put toward strengthening your financial weak link helps you increase your income potential more than any other expenditure. If you put money toward any other part of your business enterprise or toward your self-improvement as a marketable

EXAMPLE
Chain of Improvement

| Development | Product | Engagement |

Development:
Don't make enough money
Not happy with job
Don't know what to do
Don't have equipment
Don't have capital
Don't have contacts

Product:
Need more skills
Don't have degree
Not using contacts
Not fulfilling contracts
Time management
 shortfall
Financial planning
 shortfall

Engagement:
Develop connection with
 co-workers/contacts
Work on interpersonal skills
Learn about market
Respond to market

Weak link: __Development__

Possible actions to strengthen weak link:
1. Go to career counselor
2. Get books on career decisions
3. Volunteer in areas of work that look interesting
4. Try to expand a hobby into a business

Chain of Improvement

| Development | Product | Engagement |

Weak link: _____

Possible actions to strengthen weak link:

1.

2.

3.

4.

employee, then you will not move as quickly or effortlessly toward your holisticgoal. You must strengthen your weak link first to increase your capacity for earning income. For that reason, you want to free up as much money as possible to address that weak link.

So if you allocate money toward addressing your financial weak link before you allocate money for other expenses, then you have set the priority for what is most important. Most expenses that we feel are necessary are often not as necessary as we initially think, or are not necessary at the level we have been planning them. We can often lower those expenses with little hardship, given some creativity. However, we are likely to do that only if we are convinced that such sacrifices will really make a difference. By determining the weak link first, you have fulfilled that psychological need.

session I-4: making preliminary allocation of expenses

Once you have determined what your weak link is, you now know what expenses will help you generate the most additional income. In Holistic Management jargon, these expenses are wealth-generating. The other categories of expenses are inescapable expenses (debt or any other expense that you feel morally obligated to pay) and maintenance (any expense that doesn't directly generate income).

Really consider where each of your expenses fall, because you may think that many of your expenses are absolutely necessary or inescapable when they really are maintenance expenses that can be reduced or eliminated. Look back at what you spent 10 years ago. Most people lived on far less than they do now and inflation isn't the main reason for increased expenses. Rather, our expenses often rise to meet our income and that affects our ability to create profit far more than inflation or such economic phenomena as recessions or even depressions.

By determining what expenses truly are inescapable (see previous definition), you make sure you don't tinker with these—they have to be paid. However, once you determine that a particular expense is a maintenance expense, you can figure out how to reduce it because it is only maintaining your standard of living, not generating wealth or fulfilling an obligation.

Once you have categorized all your expenses into wealth-generating, inescapable, and maintenance expenses, determine which of the wealth-generating expenses need 100% allocation. For example, if you have identified that you need additional training because your "product" is the weakest link in your "chain of improvement," then you need to allocate the full amount of money for the class or training that will help to build your skills. Otherwise, it won't happen. All the rest of the wealth-generating expenses are important, but the amounts allocated to them vary. If, for example, you decide that marketing is your weakest link and you want to allocate some money toward advertising your enterprise, you might be able to adjust that figure more in the final stages of planning. In this category you have more room for negotiation because you can advertise for $35 or $3500 depending on your creativity and marginal reaction. Make sure you record all expense figures on supporting worksheets so they'll be handy when you create your plan.. Use exercise 8-6 on the next page to get you started, then see Appendix 5 for a blank worksheet.

exercise 8-6.	Below is a list of some expense items and how you could categorize them. The wealth-generating category is the only category where you will differentiate between the 100% allocation items and the partial allocation items, as in the examples below. Use the space provided below the samples to decide where all your expenses go. Use old budgets, credit card statements, and checkbooks to figure out your expense categories over the last several years.		
categorizing expenses			
purpose:	**Wealth-generating**	**Inescapable**	**Maintenance**
practice categorizing expenses	*Examples:* Training (100%) Reference books (100%)	*Examples:* Credit card debt (minimum payment) Student loan Loan from parents	*Examples:* Food Mortgage/rent Entertainment

session I-5: brainstorming ways to cut expenses

Now that you have a sense of how you want to spend your money, it's time to think about how you can cut your expenses to free up money to create more profit. You might choose later to put that profit toward some of the things you currently spend money on, but you will have already created that profit first instead of spending it and assuming you'll have the money later.

exercise 8-7. brainstorming expense-reducing ideas **Purpose:** reducing expenses	1) List all your ideas for reducing expenses below. 2) Draw a line through each item that is ridiculous or not in line with your holisticgoal. 3) Calculate what your expense totals would be if you implement the remaining ideas.

It is not economical to go to bed early to save candles when the results are twins.

—Chinese proverb

Using the same brainstorming process as before, you now brainstorm ways to cut expenses. Make sure you include outside help, again with no editing or criticism. Try for 100 ideas (but keep it speedy and silly), then go through the testing process to make sure that everyone has ownership in the ideas that you decide to try. If you have a hard time getting started, look up *The Tightwad Gazette* listed in Appendix 2. It's packed with money-saving ideas.

phase II: create your plan

- Plan Income
- Plan Profit
- Plan Expenses
- Adjust the Plan

Now that you've finished all the preliminary work it's time to create your plan. All your supporting figures should be on the worksheets you generated as part of the preliminary planning. So transfer those figures from your worksheets to the spreadsheet (see Appendix 5 for a blank sheet). Start with the Income columns on the left and give yourself room for an Income Total column before starting to list your expense columns. Create columns that make sense to you. Your worksheets for each column can include any additional subcategories that you need to keep track of. For example, if you have a category that covers communication expenses, your supporting worksheet can separate out local phone charges, long distance phone charges, Internet Service Provider charges, postage, etc.)

The next steps are a little more challenging because you must determine if all figures will work out. If your income doesn't cover the profit and expenses planned , then you have to adjust your figures to make the plan really work—including the profit you want.

session II-1: planning the income

Now that you have the spreadsheet columns set up, take all the figures from your income worksheets and enter them on the spreadsheet in Appendix 5. Review the figures and the total income they will generate.

session II-2: planning the profit

You need to plan your profit before you allocate your expenses to really challenge your preconceived notions of the amount of profit you can create. Once you really identify how this profit can help you create the life you want, you can develop a plan that will help you accomplish it. Some people might want to set aside 50% of their income as profit; others might find that figure too challenging. So find a figure that challenges you but doesn't seem overwhelming or impossible. You might also decide to subtract your debt from your income right from the start and then decide how much of your remaining income you want to put toward profit. By deciding on a set figure, you are more able to reach that target than if you assume or hope that you will have some profit at the end of the year.

To make sure that you set this profit aside as profit each month, record it in an expense column headed "planned profit" on the spreadsheet. Put it in front of all the other expenses so you don't forget its importance. The rest of your income must now cover all the expense that you have planned. If you plan on making the level of profit you have set aside, you might need to make further adjustment in your expense allocations.

session II-3: planning the expenses

Now write all your expenses into the appropriate column on the spreadsheet. Total the figures and compare it to your income totals. If your figures still aren't matching up, it's time to adjust your expenses some more.

The first place to start with planning and adjusting expense allocations is your maintenance expenses. If you can't cut maintenance expenses enough to achieve your profit then it is likely that your planned profit is too high. You don't want to get into the trap of reducing your wealth-generating expenses as it will reduce your ability to increase your income. After exploring all your options, make final adjustments and record the figures on the spreadsheet.

session II-4: adjusting the plan

If total expenses still exceed the total income figure, you've got to go back to the drawing board (increase your income, decrease your maintenance expenses, and/or reduce your profit). If you have looked at all of these categories and still can't get your plan to work, then consider decreasing your wealth-generating expenses. Don't even think about your inescapables as something you can tinker with. You should be able to make your plan work without adjusting those. Don't go on to the next step until you have a plan in which the total income exceeds total expenses.

Now that you have totals that match up, you can take a step back and look at the whole picture of your plan and, in particular, the cash flow. Will certain months bring you little income or many expenses? You still have a problem if you have a month that results in a cash flow deficit (more expenses than income in a given month) even if you have a positive balance at the end of the year. You need to plan how you will handle that situation before it happens. Brainstorm how you can adjust the plan to reduce or eliminate that deficit by reducing an expense until you have more money coming in or can bring more money in sooner. The more you use this planning process to anticipate future challenges when you are at your best rather than when you are in crisis, the better your decisions will be.

phase III: monitor the plan

Of course, like all planning, Holistic Management® Financial Planning doesn't end here. You need to monitor your plan each month (or each week if the going is rough) to see that you are on plan, and if not to decide what steps you must take to get on plan again. As you can see from the sample Annual Plan in Appendix 4, you subtract what you actually spent or earned from the planned total to get your monthly difference. If you had a cumulative difference the month before, you would add that to your current monthly difference for the cumulative difference to date. This figure shows you how those differences really add up and motivates you to really consider what actions you need to take to get back on course.

The control sheets can be particularly helpful for this type of refocusing (see example in Appendix 4) because they encourage accountability. Any time an expense or income column is adverse to plan, you must provide a way to bring it back to plan and decide who will make sure it happens.

It is essential to include all decision makers in this process as no one likes being the financial police. If everyone helps to create a plan, they also have the responsibility for making sure it works. Have each person take at least one column to monitor and suggest ways to bring the plan back in line if an income or expense figure is lower or higher than planned. Usually you should have your monthly figures entered within 10 days after the end of the month so you have the ability to shift your plan quickly. It's not important that you enter every penny, but it is important that you have a complete picture and everyone gets a chance to see it and review it. Lots of people can plan—it's the tenacity they exhibit in the monitoring and control process that will make the difference between a nice idea and actual profit.

As the following stories illustrate, many people have found this type of planning extremely helpful in bringing their financial situation around to where they want it to be regardless of their income bracket, profession, or level or debt.

Getting Out of Dodge

About a year after my wife Nancy and I began to explore Holistic Management, we decided to figure out where the money would come from to begin creating the quality of life we sought. Moneywise, we were doing "okay" from the standpoint of income, but we never seemed to be able to get ahead. Sound familiar? We, like so many others, were spending at the same level as our income.

So time and again, Nancy and I would sit down and try to do the financial planning. Actually, I would sit down and try to talk around Nancy doing the dishes, laundry, fielding questions from the kids, or answering the phone. Rather quickly, our planning session would be put on the back burner. This went on for over a year and the plan still wasn't even started. By ignoring the need for planning, the financial hole we were in was slowly getting deeper. We felt really stuck, unable to push through the inertia of years of not planning, to get that first financial plan written.

Then came the bolt out of the blue in the form of an article in the Holistic Management Quarterly titled "Reaping the Rewards," about a couple from Canada who did their financial planning away from home. In fact, they made it into a working vacation. This was an idea that made sense to me. But there was one big drawback. We didn't have the money to take this kind of trip.

So there we were, faced with a dilemma. We didn't have the quiet time at home to plan, or the money to get away from home to plan. So what do we do? Then it came to me, lines out of something from somewhere: "You have to spend money to make money." Nancy and I talked it over and decided the only way to break through was to "get out of Dodge City." So we took the plunge and booked a room for the upcoming Veterans Day weekend.

Packing up all the financial papers we thought we would need, we set off for our rendezvous with destiny. Ninety miles later, we pulled up to the motel (one of only three open at this time of year) that we'd picked blindly from the Yellow Pages. I should also add that price was a consideration in the selection. Cheap is what we needed. And the room lived up to the price. Now it was time to get to work.

The first thing to do was to find out where all the money was going. In our case, we sorted all of our canceled checks from almost a year into categories, on a month-by-month basis. When this task was completed, we then took the monthly average for the entire year. These were the base figures we started with.

Our next step was to plan our profit and the following year's financial planning trip. We took a percentage of our net income (after taxes) per month and set it aside for profit, as well as an amount for next year's trip.

Then we figured out what the fixed expenses were—things like property taxes, car insurance, etc. Also, debt service was figured here. For debt service, we chose a figure that would allow us to attain the part of our holisticgoal that stated we would be "debt free" in as short a time as we felt comfortable with.

Now the real fun began. After subtracting the fixed expenses, debt service, profit, and next year's planning trip from the net income, we had a figure to work with to cover costs of food, utilities, clothing, gasoline, car payments, etc.—all the "variables." As you can probably guess, our spending in these areas equaled more than we had money for. It was hard to decide where to make the necessary cuts, but we finally arrived at amounts that we could live with. We had a plan!

One of the things we did to help us in this process was to open a second checking account, we called "the fixed account." For any of the expenses that aren't due monthly, we went ahead and figured out a monthly payment and deposited it in the "fixed account" each month. Since the fixed expenses don't actually come every month, we were beginning to see a positive bank balance. This gave us a psychological boost. A bank balance in the black leads to a positive mind set, which makes it easier to continue the process. Another thing we did was to set up a simple spreadsheet on the computer to help us track (monitor) all the expenses on a monthly basis. (It also makes next year's financial planning a breeze!).

Another suggestion is to be flexible. An example of this would be car payments. We are currently paying on two cars, both payments being about equal. Soon, one of them will be paid off. At that point, we plan on doubling up our payments on the second car. When this car is paid off, we will continue to put aside that payment every month in the fixed account and let it build up. It wouldn't take long before we have a healthy down payment for another car. Don't be afraid to show a little financial flexibility. Your plan is not cast in concrete.

In short, the Holistic Management® Financial Planning process works. We have a working plan with the profit built in. It is a tough process to get started, but after two years, we have gained a tremendous amount of ground on our financial situation. Our last two planning sessions were spent in one of the finest Bed and Breakfasts, with dining at its most luxurious—all because we had planned for this expense.

Bill Harnach

High School Teacher
Owner, Great Basin Botanicals
Sattley, CA

Standard of Living

When I talk to people about Holistic Management, one of the things that I make sure to explain when we come to the financial planning section is the difference between quality of life and standard of living. A lot of people confuse the two, figuring that the higher their standard of living is the more quality of life they will have. But you can spend an awful lot of money trying to increase your standard of living without increasing your quality of life. In fact, you can damage your quality of life by trying to attain a standard of living you really can't afford. Of course your standard of living is important to your quality of life, but it really is just a subcategory of your quality of life. I think that's the good thing about Holistic Management. It helps you see where your standard of living comes into play within your quality of life, without confusing the two.

Leonard Pigott

Holistic Management® Certified Educator Kindersley, Saskatchewan, Canada

More May Not be Better

Last winter we developed a monthly cash flow problem. Using the cause and effect test we searched for the basis of this situation. We realized that we really needed to stay on top of monitoring. In the past, when we needed more money, we would try to find more income or would increase our debt. We were both raised with a strong mid-western work ethic that says, "If you just work harder, things will work out." Working to the point of exhaustion does not help create our holisticgoal. Using the testing questions, we analyzed our income-generating enterprises. Although more income would be nice, we figured we were doing the best we could.

Generating more income was not the answer, and we felt that our spending was under control. Still we needed a cushion with some flexibility. Our focus turned to the amount of debt service we were paying. We looked for a way to transfer wealth from one asset to another without affecting our net worth. I hoard money and, for me, taking money out of savings is downright painful. Mike helped me to see that transferring funds from an account that was not performing well to pay off the second home mortgage would not reduce our net worth nor damage our ability to generate additional wealth through investments. Taking this action pumped $200 a month into our cash flow, giving us the relief we desired.

The "no new debt policy" and the deep cuts in our spending will enable us to eliminate the rest of our credit card debt. Never before have we felt so in control of our finances and so positive about the future. Our holisticgoal is no longer a nebulous thing far off on the horizon. We are realizing it today!

Cindy Dvergsten
Holistic Management® Certified Educator
Dolores, CO

after the maiden voyage

where do you go from here?

Learning or improving any skill requires continual practice. Any athlete who wants to improve her performance will work with a coach, try new techniques, and refine old ones. But many of us operate under the myth that by the time you are 30, you should know most of what you need to know so you can coast from here on out. In other words, it should all be smooth sailing.

But most of us find that this is not the case, especially if we want to explore new territory or use different vessels, equipment, or crew to travel over old territory. With Holistic Management, you now have a new set of sails. As you go on your journey, you will increase your ability to use this tool whether that means revising your holisticgoal, sharing this information with others, creating and monitoring many plans with many people, or becoming involved with the management of other wholes. With that increased knowledge and experience you will keep this process alive and interesting, not something that is static or rote. And sharing in that learning with others will increase the chance that we can create the lives we want.

Holistic Management International can assist you in that ongoing learning. HMI is a clearinghouse for various training opportunities, produces publications and a website (www.holisticmanagement.org) for ongoing learning, and administers a free electronic discussion list for Holistic Management practitioners. To subscribe, address an email to: hmi@holisticmanagement.org (no message needed). HMI also has an updated list of Holistic Management® Certified Educators who can offer additional training and assistance, a list of various groups or branches comprised of practicing holistic managers throughout the world, and information about people who are involved in projects where they use Holistic Management as one tool to get results.

learning is a lifelong gift

So get curious and learn more about the issues, people, plants, economies, animals, and soil that impact and influence your whole. If you don't like to read, talk to local experts about these subjects and then begin to experiment. The only truly regrettable mistake is one that you don't learn from. Holistic Management isn't about not making mistakes. It is about minimizing them and trying to catch them as quickly as possible and

key concepts in this chapter

learning is a lifelong gift

get involved

All the world is full of suffering, it is also full of overcoming it.

—Helen Keller

using that information for making better decisions next time. In other words, it's about learning.

> *Until one is committed, there is hesitancy, the chance to draw back, always ineffectiveness. Concerning all acts of initiative (and creation), there is only one elementary truth, the ignorance of which kills countless ideas and splendid plans: that the moment one definitely commits oneself, then providence moves too.*
>
> *All sorts of things occur to help one that would never otherwise have occurred. A whole stream of events issues from the decision, raising in one's favor all manner of unforeseen incidents and meetings and material assistance, which no man could have dreamed would have come his way.*
>
> *Whatever you can do, or dream you can, begin it.*
>
> *Boldness has genius, power and magic in it.*
>
> *Begin it now.*
>
> Johan Wolfgang von Goethe

The reason that mistakes are seen as bad is because we have a preconceived notion about success. Success is, or so the story goes, where every decision is right, no problems arise, and we get the results we were expecting. In other words, success is about being perfect.

But life isn't like that, with or without Holistic Management. In many cases, when we have indeed made progress, other "problems" crop up. Whether we have weeds where there was bare ground or more spoken conflict but better communication, life rarely follows a straight path. And the funny thing about mistakes is that they can help us look deeper at what is happening than if we have been "successful" from the beginning. They are the fodder for deeper learning and understanding.

Mistakes aren't the problem, in fact they are often the answer. The key lies in looking at the mistake with curiosity and wonder, not fear and embarrassment. The first promotes learning, the second promotes more problems or a sense of feeling stuck. If we can nurture an environment of questioning rather than criticism, we can teach ourselves to appreciate our own efforts and the efforts of others so that we can support each other's learning rather than get mired in our discomfort or revel in that of others. For an exercise to do when an unexpected emergency pops up or a plan doesn't go according to plan, see "Simple Appreciation" (a9-1) in Appendix 1.

I will act as if what I do makes a difference.

—William James

learn with others

Many people who continue to build momentum in their lives through Holistic Management are either involved in a "management" club, a "learning" group, or a project in which Holistic Management is one of the guiding processes used. Think about the various ways in which you can engage your neighbors or community so that you can keep learning and get the outside support and interaction necessary. But above all, think about what will make this process alive and fun. As you come up with new stories and exercises, send them to us.

David Irvine, a workshop leader and management consultant, tells the story of a Seattle businessman, Don Bennett, who was the first amputee ever to climb Mount Rainier—14,410 feet—on one leg and two crutches. When asked the most important lesson he learned from his celebrated achievement, Bennett replied without hesitation, "You can't do it alone."

Rome Wasn't Built in a Day

We meet over Thanksgiving weekend each year to report on the season's activity and summarize our gains and losses and lessons. We revisit our goal and plan for the next year. In January we have our financial planning meeting and outline the budget for the new year/season. These two meetings held at the down time of our activity are held in a central location so that all members of the family can attend. We like to go to a place that makes our time together fun for everyone as well as fulfilling as we share the results of our season's labors.

We have periodic family meetings as circumstance and the need for better communication demands. These meetings often include a mealtime, and are coordinated with children's naptime or children sleeping over at a cousin's house in order to facilitate the quiet time for the adults to talk. We have instigated a voice mailbox for our family to use so we can share information with everyone at the same time. This saves the frustration of thinking you have told everyone that a dinner meeting is planned for Thursday night only to be told Thursday afternoon, "I didn't know anything about any meeting and I have other plans!"

Where we have our breakdowns is when we think perfection is the only acceptable level of attainment, and we are all so far from it! The challenge to work out of old paradigms, use creativity instead of money, think of the whole instead of parts, build up others while being patient with yourself, besides remembering to fix the chicken house door, order feed, market new products, etc. That kind of life calls for a definite learning curve and the realization that Rome was not built in a day!

Kay James
Co-owner of James Ranch, Durango, Colorado

In his travels around North America as a teacher and consultant to family businesses, Irvine has met many individuals who have attended Holistic Management courses. Invariably, he notes, "These individuals come home from these courses excited and enriched. But all too often they attempt to go it alone and end up frustrated and discouraged. Some even try to work alone within their own family.

"Unless that initial energy is nurtured and supported, Holistic Management can become overwhelming. The key to cultivating and sustaining that energy is 1) ongoing support, and 2) continuous learning. It is critical to have these two elements in place following any course and there is no better tool for providing them than management clubs [support groups]. Where management clubs are working effectively, Holistic Management is thriving."

Sure, learning to think holistically, make decisions holistically, and plan holistically can be challenging. But after experiencing the thrill of really seeing a situation clearly or making decisions that truly move you in the direction you want to go, the world will never be the same.

Guidelines For Creating an Effective Support Group

1)   Don't Force It!

Allow your club to emerge rather than try to force it. Not everyone is ready for or needs a formal management club. Put an invitation out, perhaps several times. But remember, when the readiness is there, people will come—and not before. This may mean that your club will initially include only two families, or maybe even only you and your significant other. It's better that two families meet consistently every month in a meaningful way, than 10 families that meet a couple times a year on a superficial level.

2)   Clarify Your Purpose and Expectations

As soon as possible take time as a group to create a statement of purpose (why you are getting together), what your expectations are for the group, and what sort of meeting/learning environment you want to create. An example might be:

Purpose: To create a supportive learning community in which we can share our successes and setbacks in practicing Holistic Management.

Expectations: To increase our understanding and better our practice of Holistic Management, move closer to the holisticgoals we have set as families or businesses, and gain meaningful support for our efforts.

Environment: To create an atmosphere of openness and trust (where all feel free to express themselves) and get-togethers that are so much fun and so informative that we will want to keep meeting forever.

3)   Establish Limits

Limit the numbers in your group. When you have a goal of creating a climate of trust where people can feel safe to give and receive meaningful support, I have found it is best to limit your group to less than 24 people. Trust, openness, and honesty are necessary components to a well-functioning community and need a "container" in which to build. If new people come and go, the club tends to become a "cocktail party" rather than a "learning community" because trust, in particular, only builds over time.

4)   Challenge Yourselves

Do something as a group that you don't do in your regular meetings, at least once a year. We have found that unless we get out of our comfort zone as a group, by taking a workshop that requires some risk-taking, or by having an outside facilitator encourage us to open up and share with each other, the group begins to get somewhat superficial.

5)   Teach Each Other

There is no better way to increase your understanding of Holistic Management than to teach it. If you have recently been to a course, it can be a powerful, win-win experience to come back to the group and teach them what you have learned.

6)   Maintain Balance

In order to maintain vitality and sustainability, all organizations need a balance between relationships and production. Whenever they are off balance, and one takes priority over another, the system begins to break down.

The key is to keep a balance between what I call the "head" and the "heart." Invariably, there will be both "head" and "heart" people in every management club (just as there are in every family). The only way to keep the two in balance is to monitor them constantly.

7)   Don't Rush It!

Trust the process! We have been meeting as a management club for over four years and we are just now at the point of feeling totally comfortable with each other. The level of trust and acceptance we have so carefully built has taken many meetings, many courses, and much sharing, and continues to deepen. We have had boring meetings, we have had some painful meetings, we have had exciting meetings, and we have had a lot of fun together. As Don Campbell, one of the pioneers of Holistic Management in Canada says, "Direction is more important than velocity!"

David Irvine
Author, speaker, and workshop leader
Calgary, Alberta, Canada

Two Heads Are Better Than One

We think that one of the things that holds people back from really practicing Holistic Management is a lack of understanding of the decision-making process. It's one thing to read the book or take the class, it's another to get out there and make decisions holistically. We also think it is essential to have a support group to carry the momentum of enthusiasm built up while doing a course or just having learned about Holistic Management. Support groups can also help when you have a problem you can't seem to figure out. With more experienced members or even just more people working through the process, you are bound to come up with a better decision. In turn, when you have a similar problem, then you've already been through the necessary steps and thinking so you are ahead and won't make the same mistakes.

Ian and Pam Mitchell-Innes

Ranchers
South Africa

Confessions of a Holistic Management Student

I came looking for an explanation of your process and you told me to look inside myself.

I came looking for answers and you told me to learn to ask questions.

I came to learn about your planning process and you told me to describe life 100 years from now.

I came to discuss finances and you told me to collaborate with my neighbors.

I came to learn the effects of Holistic Management on my balance sheet and you told me to draw a map of the land around me.

I came to assign a cost to practicing Holistic Management and you told me Holistic Management is free.

I came looking for economic precision and you told me to share emotions with my teammates.

I came to learn to implement and you told me to learn to be congruent.

I came with a measure of chaos, and despite the non-sense of your responses, I leave with the most meaningful hope for order I have ever known...Thank you.

Drausin Wulsin

Grass-based dairy farmer
Cincinnati, OH

appendices

appendix 1: additional exercises

<u>answer</u> to exercise 1-1 (paradigm shift) **found at the beginning of chapter 1**	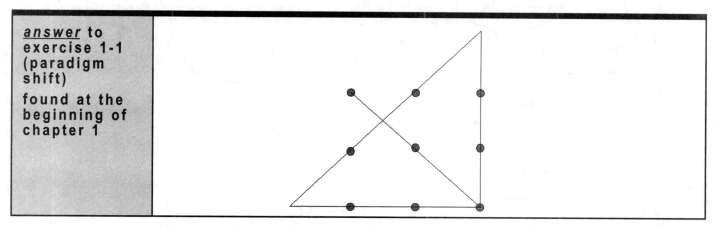

Note: The exercise numbers in this appendix include a reference to the chapter covering the subject of the exercise. The numbers are constructed as follows: a (for appendix) [chapter number] - [sequence of this exercise for this chapter within the appendix]. So—the exercise number a4-2 indicates that this is an exercise to be found in the appendix and it gives you more opportunity to practice the material in chapter 4. It is the second exercise for chapter 4 within the appendix.

exercise a1-1. **exploring beliefs** **purpose:** practice exploring underlying beliefs	1) Identify a family belief (i.e., We don't have enough time). If you are unsure where to start, look at a family struggle (We aren't getting things done that need to get done) and see what belief is behind it. 2) After identifying the family belief, begin listing all of the thoughts and emotions behind that belief. You might want to mindmap the items that come up instead of just listing them. See the example on the following page. If you get stuck, use the first set of ideas to generate a second set of ideas. Play off of your original idea. 3) As you begin listing these items, ask questions that help you understand the other family members' contributions. Don't argue or criticize anyone else's contribution. Try to get at least 10 items. 4) Now have everyone think of all the ways in which that initial belief isn't true (all the ways in which you have plenty of time) and that show the subsequent beliefs to also not be true (i.e. There are things that the grownups and kids like to do together). Again, you might want to mindmap these ideas. See the example on the following page. In answering these questions you are exploring new beliefs and behaviors that you can use to move beyond the limits that were imposed by your previous paradigm as well as acknowledging any progress you have made or things you are already doing to shift this paradigm. If you have trouble with this exercise you can always get help from a friend of the family who knows you but is outside your situation. Paradigm shifting requires keeping an open mind and looking at the belief from as many different angles as you can.

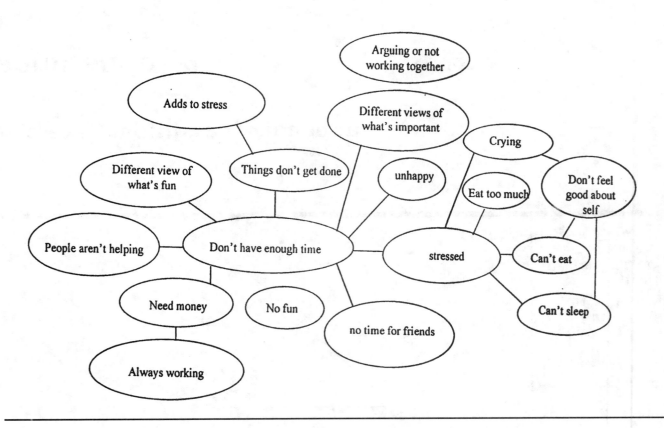

Belief

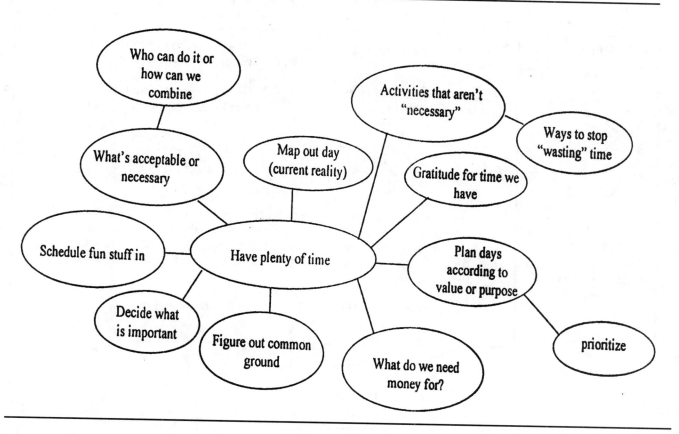

<u>Reality</u>

exercise a1-2.
holism exercise

This is an exercise to help people start to look at the world more holistically, to begin seeing more of the various relationships and interactions that surround or are a part of any person or thing. It helps people realize that nothing is in isolation. You can use the example given below to help you get started and use the space on the facing page to create your own. This is a great exercise for a vacation or commute.

1) Have a family member pick an object or person.

2) Begin to make a spiderweb or mindmap of how that object or person is related, connected, interacts, etc. with other items. Or think about what combines to make it (i.e., hydrogen and oxygen combine to make water) or how it combines with something to make something new (i.e., water is used to make soda pop).

Try this exercise several times and see if you can beat your record.

purpose:
practice looking at the world more holistically

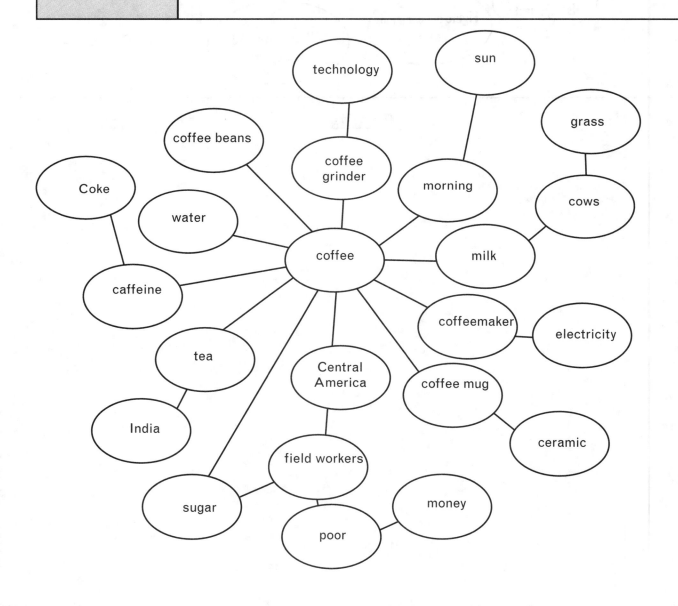

exercise a1-3

synergy

purpose:

analyze roles within your group and possibly reassign them

Use the example below to help you fill out the blank form on the facing page as you go through these steps.

1) Have each person pick a sport or group activity (like dancing, singing in a choir, acting, etc.).

2) Now have them list the role of each member of your group as if you were all engaged in the activity. For example, let's say I decide to take the game of basketball as my metaphor or activity. I would want to figure out who in our family is the coach or captain, who is a point guard or the forward or the center. Who might be the cheerleader or the fans or the manager or the trainer?

3) After you've had time to assign roles, explain your reasoning.

4) Now figure out your current "win-loss" record, score, or rating. What percentage of the time do you think you are behaving like a winning team by working together? On a scale of 1 to 10, how well are you performing?

5) Determine how you could be a better team. What positions would each member need to play? What does your win-loss record or performance need to be?

Synergy Exercise

Activity: Basketball   **Group: Family**

Person	Current position	Potential position
Mom	Cheerleader	Point guard
Dad	Coach	Center
Fred	Statistician	Forward
Sam	Point guard	Forward
Louise	Wing guard	Wing guard
Mary	Referee	Wing guard
Grandma	Manager	Fan

Current win/ lose record: 3-7   **Potential win/ lose record: 7-3**

Synergy Exercise

Activity: _____   **Group:** _____

Person   **Current position**   **Potential position**

_____   _____   _____

_____   _____   _____

_____   _____   _____

_____   _____   _____

_____   _____   _____

_____   _____   _____

_____   _____   _____

_____   _____   _____

_____   _____   _____

_____   _____   _____

Current win/ lose record: **Potential win/ lose record:**

exercise a1-4.

Identifying motivators

purpose:

practice understanding one's motivators

This is an exercise that I developed from the work on motivation done by Barbara Sher (*Live the Life You Love*) and Robert Fritz (*Corporate Tides*). Both of these authors demonstrate that if you know what motivates you, then you can use that information to create a motivating environment. With that motivating environment, people can tap their unique talents more easily and feel inspired. However, remember that you can only help create the environment, not motivate someone.

Below are two columns. The first column lists things that motivate different people. The second column lists ways that people might create an encouraging environment for a person who responds to that type of motivation.

1) Have each person pick the top five motivators for them (add any to the list that you can think of).

2) Then select the items from the second column that create a motivating environment for you.

3) Share this list with the rest of the group.

This information is very important for changing behavior. Change is often difficult, particularly with survival behavior (learned behavior to meet basic needs). If you know what creates a motivating environment, then you can use that information to encourage the new behaviors. This may not be the time to say, "But they should be intrinsically motivated." After all, there's a place for discipline and a place for creativity.

Motivator	Reward
Structure	Taking a class, Deadlines, Other people in charge
Growth	Freedom of choice, Excitement, Adventure
Money	Compensation
Symbols	Awards
Security	Continuity, Consistency, Safety
Relationships	Scolding, Guilt, Peer pressure, Teams/Teamwork
Individualism	Independence, Self-sufficiency
Career	Opportunity, Meaningful work
Spirituality/Religion	Prayer, Meditation, Positive thinking
Rewards	Money, Treats, Trophies, Stars, Gifts
Fear of Negative Consequences	Control/conflict, Change
Respect/Recognition	Praise, Responsibility
Satisfaction	Interesting work, Meaningful work
Support	Talking with others
Success	Other successes, Sense of accomplishment,
Small	Successes, Achievement, Other people's successes
Power (over others)	Revenge, Other people's failure, Sense of control
Power (under others)	Lecturing, Fear, Shaming, Policies, Rules
Challenges	Competition, Dares, Change, Learning
Status	Titles, "Fashion," Sense of worth

For example, let's say that you want to change the way you interact with your children. You realize that you are too critical and want to respond more constructively or give them positive feedback. So you look at the list and realize that the things that motivate you the most are: relationships, respect, and success. Knowing this, you then might let the rest of the family know what you are working on and see who will help you (be on your team—relationships). You might ask your team members to monitor you and to praise you when you do accomplish the task (respect) and to acknowledge any little success. In this way, you create an environment that not only motivates you, but could well motivate the rest of the group.

exercise a3-1.

asking the right questions

purpose:

to make sure you're asking the right questions

If you're exploring options and aren't at the testing stage yet, play 20 questions with yourself to determine what you know and don't know, and what information you would need to gather. It's easy to fall into the "yes, but" syndrome, which can be distracting. If you are forced to answer yes or no (as in 20 questions) you begin to think carefully about the questions you will ask.

For those unfamiliar with 20 questions, you start with one person who thinks of an animal, mineral, or vegetable but doesn't tell anyone else. The other players are allowed to ask 20 questions, to which the answer will be a "yes" or a "no," to determine the object about which the other person is thinking. The strategy is to start with more general questions and move to more specific ones. For example, if one player is thinking of an elephant, then the other person wouldn't want to ask, "Is it a car?" A more appropriate and generic first question is something like, "Is it an animal?" (or vegetable or mineral). This is really a good exercise for developing thoughtful questioning and deductive reasoning.

Once everyone has the hang of that game, you can move to logic puzzles, which is particularly fun as a group activity. You can find these kinds of puzzles in bookstores and libraries. Here's an example:

Everyday a man gets on the elevator on the 11th floor and rides down to the first floor, goes to work, comes home and rides the elevator to the 8th floor, gets off and walks up the stairs to the 11th floor. Why?

Again, the person who knows the answer can field any questions to which the answer is a "yes" or a "no." *(Answer: He is a dwarf and can only reach the button for the 8th floor).*

If you are using this type of questioning for your own situation you will be surprised at your ability to ask a series of questions to which you can answer yes or no. By framing them in "yes" or "no" questions, it makes you break your questions down into smaller bites which keeps you from confusing the issues.

For example, if you have a situation at work (or your place of worship or of recreation, etc.) where you used to feel good about a relationship you had with a person but with whom you now find yourself withdrawing, some of the questions you might ask yourself are:

- Do I want to change the relationship?

- Do I respect the person?

- Do I like the person?

- Do I trust the person?

- Do I know what I need to say?

- Do I trust myself to say what I need to say?

- If I don't trust myself, do I have someone who could help me? That I could talk to?

This kind of questioning will elicit far different answers, or at least a different knowledge of yourself, than the typical questions of why, what, when, etc. (which certainly have their uses—see the Cause and Effect test in Chapter Five).

exercise a3-2.
points of view

purpose:
practice empathy

One of the easiest ways to elicit empathy from people is to ask the question, "How would you feel if you were me (or Sue or Bob or whomever)?" If you ask that question out of curiosity rather than as an attack, most people are able to get pretty close to how you or whomever might feel. In other words, they are able to see things from a different point of view.

Note: When you are asking any type of question and you get stuck with an "I don't know," ask yourself or the other person, "If you did know...?" For example, when we decided to try a new school for our son Ben, he was able to share with us how he had been worried about the upcoming school year at his old school because of something that had taken place a month before. When we asked him what kept him from telling us how he was feeling then, he said "I don't know." Then I asked him, "If you did know, what would you say?" He replied, "If I did know, I guess it's because I was afraid you would get mad and make it worse for me."

One of the most effective exercises for learning empathy is role-playing or doing some kind of skits. This role-playing is particularly helpful for working on an ongoing situation at school or work. Try to get the characters to switch so the "victim" is the "bully" or vice versa. Talk afterwards about how you felt as you played that role. You will influence your children by your ability to enter into your role. A book that has a number of exercises for children is *Why's Everyone Always Picking on Me* by Terrence Webster-Doyle.

As you build your empathy skills and are able to see more sides of a situation, you will be better able to see the bigger picture. Jonas Salk in his book, *Anatomy of Reality,* wrote about how he tried to be a cancer cell or a virus and then put himself in the place of an immune system to figure out what questions he should ask or how to set up an experiment as he worked on vaccines.

As a warm-up to a skit you can create situations that come up in your life. Have people take turns being the family dog or the car or the computer. Pick something that has moving parts or is alive. Try to figure out what makes it tick. Ask yourself, "If I were a ...., why would I do what I do?" "How would that affect me?"

Think about the reasons why you do what you do and apply your knowledge to whatever it is you are pretending to be. That perspective will help you ask more questions to better understand those around you and how you might better engage with them.

See also the "Bridge over troubled water" exercise (a3-4).

exercise a3-3.
your turn

purpose:
finding the group's strength

This exercise is a variation of the old game "Hot Potato." In the old version of "Hot Potato," you set a timer and everyone would toss a potato around trying not to be the last one holding it when the timer went off. The new version is a combination of the old game and a variation of Edward DeBono's, creator of the "Six Hats" game from his board game, *Mindgames*.

1) Start with each person writing down any situation she can think of on a scrap of paper (try to get a total of at least 20—real or imaginary. For example, your dog attacked the neighbor).

2) Fold the papers up and drop into a hat or some other container.

3) Next, have everyone take one of the roles listed below. If you have more people than roles, that's okay because you can just have two people playing the same role. If you have fewer people than roles, it gets trickier because then you have to have some people play more than one role.

The roles are:

• Emoter-- (What feelings might be involved for all parties in the situation or are evident within the process?)

• Questioner --(What additional information is needed to better understand the situation?)

• Critic-- (What problems or unintended consequences might result from the situation?)

• Polly Anna--(What are all the possibilities and positive outcomes?)

• Assessor--(What are all the various factors involved?)

• Planner--(What are our options? Where can we go from here?)

• Observer --(This person can't have any other roles as she needs to be able to focus on the group process and report).

3) Once you have assigned roles, you might want to stick with them for a couple of rounds as this game can require a lot of concentration.

4) Get in a circle and have the observer draw the first situation out of a hat. The observer reads the situation out loud to the group and starts the timer (length of rounds can be set by the group, but you might want to limit each round to a couple of minutes).

5) After the observer starts the timer, she tosses a soft ball (like a tennis ball) to someone in the group, who must immediately respond to the situation from their role. As soon as that person finishes, he tosses the ball to someone else. You need to be aware of which roles have not responded yet and toss the ball to them. (For the first couple of rounds you can go in order around the circle.)

6) Once everyone has responded, you go around again. You are not responding in any order, but the point of the game is to see how many responses you can get before the time is up. See if you can beat your group's personal best.

7) The observer will keep track of number of responses and also will note responses to see if anyone missed her turn or if someone's response should count.

8) Allow time for discussion after each round.

This exercise helps people to recognize that we need all of these roles to maximize the group's capacity to understand and explore a given situation. You will also begin to notice which roles come most easily to some people and where others need to develop their skills. This exercise also helps people see situations as opportunities to explore many options and possibilities rather than just debating about the one right action.

exercise a3-4.

bridge over troubled water

purpose:

focusing on common ground

Constructive communication is an important piece to group decision-making because everyone needs to be able to speak and to feel heard (listened to and understood). Most conflict is the result of a breakdown in communication or an imbalance of power. But if you care deeply enough that everyone is heard, and you have a commitment to creating a plan that meets everyone's needs and interests (not necessarily their positions or agendas), you will succeed at hearing each other regardless of what technique you use. People will feel heard when they can tangibly see what they said had an impact or was implemented.

Having a holisticgoal helps to focus people on the common ground they all share because it expresses basic needs. But people often get sidetracked by other's expressions of their position or desire for certain tools to be used. An adult child might say to an elderly parent, "You need to be in a nursing home" as opposed to "I'm worried about you and I want you to be healthy and safe. I also don't want the stress of wondering if you are okay." Likewise, the elderly parent might respond, "I want to live in my own home" as opposed to "I want to be healthy; I want freedom; and I don't want you to worry about me." The idea of using a bridge as a metaphor for common ground within a conflict came from a training session Dr. Sandra Starr facilitated. Using the bridge illustration at the bottom of the facing page as an example, follow the steps below.

1) In the picture of the bridge at the top of the page, write a current conflict (e.g., housing arrangements for an elderly parent) below the bridge.

2) On one side write the one person's positions (her reasons).

3) On the other side, write the other person's positions.

4) On the support wires of the bridge write each person's interests. You can get to the underlying interests by exploring the various position statements. Interest statements are more about feelings and values (see the example below).

5) Above the bridge, write the values that underlie the interests with which probably neither party would disagree. This is your common ground.

6) From this common ground, come to a solution where you meet those needs without miring in the specific conditions. That is the bridge over troubled waters.

If you have trouble getting to the other person's underlying values, follow these steps:

a) When the other person explains his position, repeat back what you thought he said, and ask any questions you have for clarification. Ask if your summary is correct. If it is, proceed to step (b), otherwise repeat step (a). Never interrupt (write down your thoughts on a piece of paper so you can ask your questions after he is done or to help you remember what he said).

b) Ask any other questions that you need to ask to better understand his position and the values that underpin it. From the information you have gathered, determine what you think the underlying values are if the other person has not been able to articulate them. Ask the other person if what you said was true. If it is, proceed to step (c), otherwise, repeat steps (a) or (b).

c) Ask him what he would like to have as a solution. Again make sure that you understood what he said.

d) Ask him, "If you were me, how would you feel about that solution?"

e) Tell him what underlies your position (think values).

f) Offer your solution

g) Tie the discussion into your group's holisticgoal, if there is one in that situation, or to your own (in your mind) if there isn't a group one.

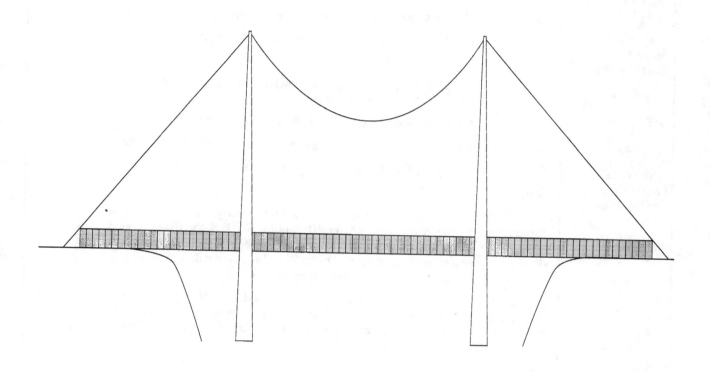

Conflict Resolution Bridge

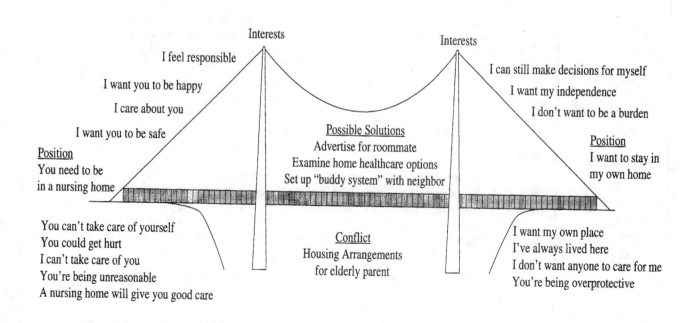

Interests

I feel responsible

I want you to be happy

I care about you

I want you to be safe

Interests

I can still make decisions for myself

I want my independence

I don't want to be a burden

Possible Solutions
Advertise for roommate
Examine home healthcare options
Set up "buddy system" with neighbor

Position
You need to be
in a nursing home

Position
I want to stay in
my own home

You can't take care of yourself
You could get hurt
I can't take care of you
You're being unreasonable
A nursing home will give you good care

Conflict
Housing Arrangements
for elderly parent

I want my own place
I've always lived here
I don't want anyone to care for me
You're being overprotective

exercise a5-1.

values clarification survey

purpose:

practice in setting a holisticgoal

Step One

Take 20-30 minutes to answer the following questions:

1) What makes you happy now or has made you happy?

2) What is most important to you?

3) If you had to list the five most important times of your life, what would they be? What made them so pivotal?

4) What do you dream about? What do you hope for?

5) What three factors in your life keep you from living the life you want?

6) What are your five greatest talents or assets?

Step Two

Using the answers to these questions, extract from your statements all the values represented in the responses. After 10 minutes, look at the list of your values. Now attempt the "six levels of why." Pick the first value and decide why you value it. Now decide why you value that answer. Try another layer after that, and another. Try to get down six layers to discover what your core values are.

For example, let's say you value health. Why? Maybe because you value independence. Why? Because you value responsibility. Why? Because you value integrity. If you continue this line of questioning you will better understand why different values are important to you.

Step Three

Now it's time to write your quality of life statement. On paper, describe the life you want to lead in the whole you are managing. Try to keep the description as "essential" as possible (i.e. rather than say "to build a straw bale house" phrase it instead something like, "build a house out of environmentally appropriate building materials"). Try to give as much detail as possible; describe what you want your life to be like on a daily basis. Focus on internal as well as external attributes of the life you want to lead. Check to make sure those things you value (refer to survey) are in your description.

Step Four

The next section is the forms of production. Think about all you have written as your "quality of life." What do you have to produce materially as well as interpersonally in order to create them? For example, if you said time with your family was important to you then you must produce the time to spend with your family members. Other "forms of production" may include things like "a debt-free life,: "open communication with my neighbors," " a steady income," "trust in my co-workers," "a healthy lifestyle," "a sense of inner peace," etc. Keep it essential (i.e. income from the land versus income from tomatoes). Go down six levels; why do you need to produce that?

Step Five

The last section is your future resource base. What do you need to do to sustain these forms of production, and thus your quality of life, over time? Look at who and what currently supports you now. Make sure you include these things in your assessment as they will have to be in the future. Don't forget your health. Don't forget nature, the surrounding landscape, and the natural resources you need. Also consider things like services (health clinic, good schools, etc.) or community resources.

Congratulations! You have a holisticgoal to test your decisions toward.

This exercise was developed by Holistic Management® Certified Educator Kate Brown.

exercise a5-2. **defining your future** **(or playing game show host of "This is Your Life")** **purpose:** **clarify what you want in life**	Pretend that you are the game show host of "This is Your Life." The person being honored is 100-year-old you. That's right, you are 100 years old. ● What have you done? ● How have you lived your life? ● What do people think about you? This game show host knows it all, has done all the research. He's talked to your friends, family, and colleagues/peers. ● What did they say? ● Where are you living? Write as if you are the game show host (Joe graduated from high school with honors in 2001). When everyone is finished writing down their ideas (or drawing pictures or dictating), have someone else read what you wrote. After everyone has had a chance to read, see if there are any common traits that you all feel are important (honesty, respect, responsibility, etc.). Make a list. Consider such questions as: ● What type of people would you spend most of your time with if those values interest you? ● When might you spend time with people who don't share your values or beliefs? ● What would the surrounding community and land look like because of your actions?

exercise 5-3. **the tree of life** **purpose:** **visual illustration of a holisticgoal**	Those of you more visually oriented might prefer Holistic Management® Certified Educator Rio de la Vista's idea of the tree of life as a metaphor for the holisticgoal. (The illustrations on the next two pages are by Jane Reed.) In the first example, the trunk of the tree is the "whole being managed." The leaves and the fruit are the quality of life, which tends to change over time. The leaves are connected to the trunk and supported by the branches, which are the forms of production, the ways you as an individual or a group create the quality of life you want. Finally, though we cannot see the roots of a tree, we know that its life depends upon them. Likewise, we cannot see the future, but we know that the well-being of the future resource base will determine the long-term well-being of our lives and those of future generations. With that in mind, look at the blank sample provided. Fill in the sections of the tree as you see them fitting together given the discussions you have had about your values, what you want your life to be like, and what you have to do to produce it.

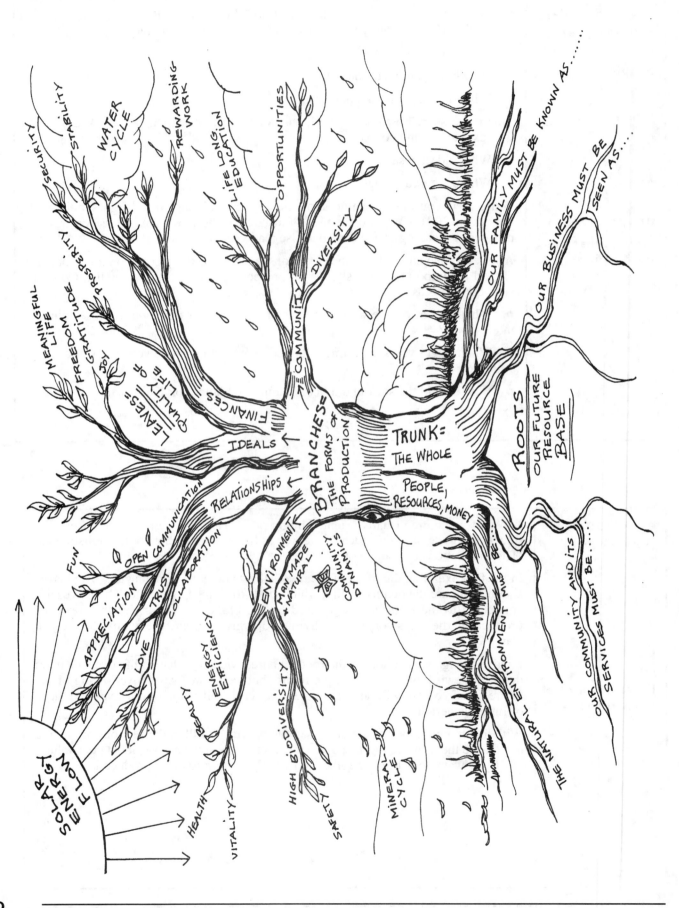

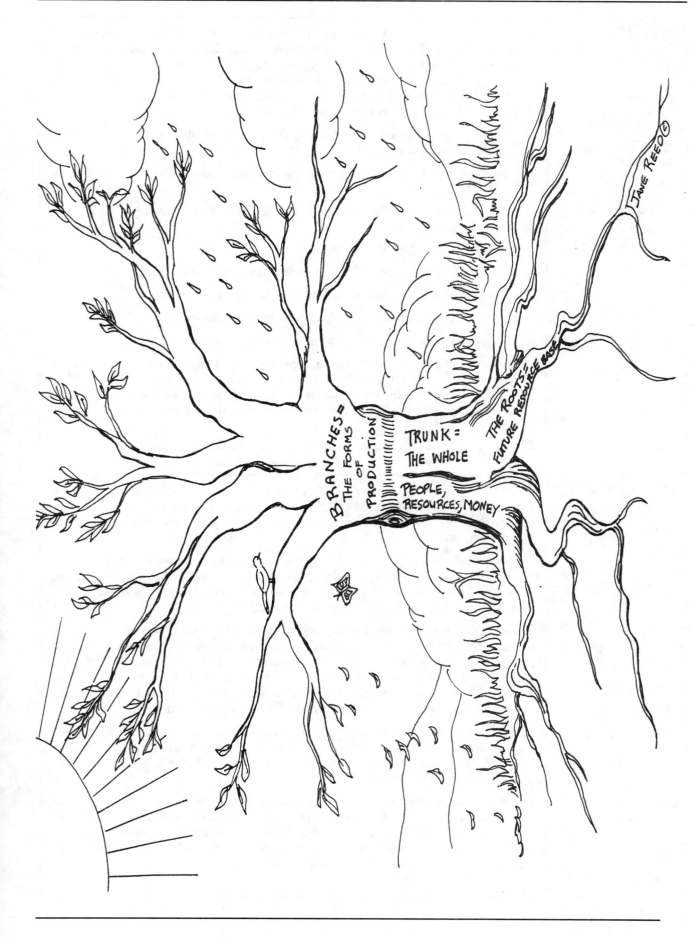

BRANCHES = THE FORMS OF PRODUCTION

TRUNK = THE WHOLE

PEOPLE, RESOURCES, MONEY

THE ROOTS = FUTURE RESOURCE BASE

JANE REED©

exercise a6-1.

the tester

purpose:

a way to remember the testing questions

This exercise is a variation of a gift that members of the Colville Confederated Tribes gave to participants at a training session I attended. They made this gift for us to represent the testing questions and to help us remember to test our decisions. Use whatever colors seem appropriate to you. I've just suggested these colors as an example. The important thing is to decide what helps people remember the different tests. You can use any material with any design.

1) Decide what item you would most likely carry around or wear (key chain, bracelet, necklace, money clip, etc.).

2) Assign a color for each test, something that you equate with the different tests. For example:

● Cause and Effect = Blue (for water and the idea of concentric circles moving out from the root cause)

● Sustainability = Yellow (for the sun)

● Energy/Money Source and Use = Green (for money and natural resources)

● Weak Link = Black (like a black hole as it stops progress)

● Marginal Reaction = Gray (helps you figure out that gray area of priorities)

● Society and Culture = Red (for emotion and the heart)

Kids can participate in this exercise, whether they string colored beads, color a piece of paper, or cut out construction paper. If you have an idea of what you'd like to make, but aren't sure how to make it, there are lots of books at your public library on handicrafts, and most hobby stores carry the supplies for making these items.

exercise a6-2.

natural resource inventory

purpose:

understanding where manufactured goods come from and what you depend on

This exercise helps if you have family/group members who are a little fuzzy about where objects or manufactured goods come from or who don't see why they should be interested in how natural resources are used, obtained, etc. It is also a good warm-up for the DegenGenRegen exercise in Chapter Six.

1) Have each person pick a room in your home and list everything that is in the room or that makes up the room (you can pair up a younger child with an older one as needed). You can set a time limit if your rooms contain a lot of items (which can be an interesting observation in and of itself).

2) After they've listed the items, you can get together as a group or individually decide which natural resource is used to make each item or involves the use of a natural resource (i.e. a metal faucet with plastic pipe transports water for drinking and washing). You can do a two-step breakdown, if needed, for items like window=glass=sand, etc. (There is a breakdown of typical items in the Natural Resource Calculation section in Appendix 3 if you need it.)

3) Now check the Natural Resource Calculation section in Appendix 3 to estimate how much electricity or water various appliances use, what products are made from which resources, and where you can find out more information about understanding your natural resource use.

Without an understanding of what your natural resource use is you can't make decisions towards your holisticgoal because you don't have the information or knowledge of what the impact of your decisions are on the environment. Since the environment's health directly relates to economic and social sustainability, this information helps you be an informed consumer.

exercise a6-3. testing decisions	This is a good exercise do while traveling or while you are waiting in an office. It helps you develop the skill of testing a decision towards your holisticgoal and can be quite thought provoking. There are two ways to do this exercise, but if people are still fuzzy about the testing questions, it's good to have your "tester" (a6-1) with you: (Version 1) You test all your decisions toward the family's holisticgoal. In this case each family member has a turn to come up with a scenario or a current situation where one family member or the whole family has to make a decision. You can come up with some pretty outrageous situations with which to test each other or take the time to consider current situations. or
purpose: practice testing your decisions	(Version 2) Define a new whole from any point of history (i.e. you are a runaway slave). In this exercise you have to set up a quick holisticgoal (you'll notice it probably won't be that different from the one you have now since most people have the same basic values and want the same basic things). But in this version, you also might want to take the time to figure out what resources you have available (you can't make a quick getaway in a car). This exercise is particularly fun when you get the whole group engaged with everyone taking on different roles. You still take turns coming up with new situations you must face (You are hungry and can't find food, etc.) and acting as a referee as to whether or how your decisions are moving you toward your holisticgoal.

**exercise
a9-1.**

**simple
appreciation**

purpose:

**use this as
one way to
cope well
with the
unexpected**

This exercise is useful when coping with unexpected events or emergencies. It may seem simplistic, but it helps to identify what direction you want to move and the factors that you need to consider. In essence, it is a simple appreciation of the situation that helps you substitute routine for panic.

1) Define the objective or result that you want in one paragraph. Keep it succinct.

2) List all the aspects of the situation. Try to think of any information that affects the situation. Don't worry about order; just brainstorm a list.

3) Outline several courses of action (You can develop as many variations of a plan as you want to suit your situation).

4) Pick the best plan.

For example, we had a sudden change in Ben's schooling one year that prompted some quick decisionmaking. Less than a week away from the beginning of the school year, I noticed an article in the paper about an alternative school starting in our area. We went to the meeting, liked what we saw, but there were so many logistics to consider: we weren't sure if this school would make it, we had a non-refundable deposit at the other school, we hadn't planned for this extra responsibility in our schedules, etc.

It was easy to feel overwhelmed by all the considerations and fall back to the less risky choice even though we weren't happy with that situation (which was the primary reason for having looked in the paper for another school). But, when we sat down and did the simple appreciation, it became apparent which information we needed to help us make the decision (more information on the school and talking with friends to help with scheduling, etc.) By writing down all the factors, we were able to gain clarity on how much risk was involved, how much the new opportunity filled needs that the old school didn't, and basically clarified what the best plan was for us with a minimal amount of stress and worry about whether the decision was right or not.

Use the space below or a separate sheet of paper and follow steps 1 through 4 above, using a recent emergency or surprise situation in your life.

Objective or result:

The situation:

Alternative courses of action:

Best plan:

appendix 2

resources of interest

The resources listed in this appendix have been useful to others in learning and practicing Holistic Management.

For a more comprehensive annotated bibliography that particularly addresses the concerns of those running a business or managing land, see *Holistic Management: A New Framework for Decision-Making* by Allan Savory with Jody Butterfield.

games and songs

The Optical Illusion Book, by Seymour Simon. NY: William Morrow and Co., 1984.

> Provides examples of optical illusion that help you practice shifting your paradigms.

Rise Up Singing, edited by Peter Blood and Annie Patterson

> A great folk song book with 1200 songs. Below is a list of songs that are particularly helpful for teaching different concepts (and are fun to sing). If you haven't heard the song before, this book lists the recordings on which they were released.

"There's a Hole in the Bucket" (Cause and Effect)

"I Know an Old Lady" (Cause and Effect)

"There's a Hole in the Bottom of the Sea" (Holism)

"The Green Grass Grows All Around" (Holism)

"The Riddle Song" (Paradigms)

"When I'm Gone" (Decisions)

"Turn, Turn, Turn" (Time/Life)

"Never Turning Back" (Inspiration)

"Safe in the Harbor" (Journey and Dreams)

"Come Fare Away With Me" (Journey)

"The Bread Song" (Where food comes from)

"What You Do With What You've Got" (Attitude)

"A Place in the Choir" (Contributions to the Group)

Silver Bullets, by Karl Rohnke. Hamilton, MA: Project Adventure, 1984.

A great resource for puzzles and all sorts of experiential learning.

the environment

Across Time and Space: Ecosystem Management, by the Soil and Water Conservation Society

Well done cartoon booklet helping kids learn why everyone has to understand ecosystem processes and how they can help create healthy ecosystems.

The Ages of Gaia: A Biography of Our Living Earth, by James Lovelock. NY: WW Norton and Co., 1988.

Alternative Energy Sourcebook, edited by John Schaeffer. Ukiah, CA: Real Goods Trading Corporation, 1996.

Earth in the Balance, by Al Gore. NY: Houghton-Mifflin Co, 1992..

The Ecology of Commerce, by Paul Hawken. NY: Random House, 1993.

The Essential Whole Earth Catalogue: Access to Tools and Ideas. NY: Doubleday and Co., 1986.

A Green History of the World: The Environment and the Collapse of Great Civilizations, by Clive Ponting. NY: St. Martin's Press, 1991.

Holistic Management: A New Framework for Decision-Making, by Allan Savory and Jody Butterfield. Washington, DC: Island Press, 1999.

Written by the co-founders of Holistic Management International. It is *the* definitive, very readable explanation of Holistic Management practice and its evolution.

How to Grow More Vegetables, by John Jeavons. Ten Speed Press, 1995.

Humanure: A Guide to Composting Human Manure, by Joseph Jenkins. Chelsea Green Pub. Co., 1996.

Introduction to Permaculture, by Bill Mollison and Reny Slay. Ten Speed Press, 1997.

Living by Design: Ecology and the Making of Sustainable Places, by Sim Van Der Ryn and Stuart Cowan. Covelo, CA: Island Press, 1995.

The Lorax (book and video), by Dr. Suess. NY: Random House, 1971.

Great book to start a discussion on sustainability

The Machinery of Nature: The Living World Around Us and How it Works, by Paul Ehrlich. NY: Simon and Schuster, 1981.

Natural Capitalism, by Paul Hawken, Amory Lovins, and Hunter Lovins. NY: Little and Brown, 1999.

The Natural House, by David Pearson. NY: Simon and Schuster, 1989.

The One-Straw Revolution, by Masanobu Fukuoka. Emmaus: Rodale Press, 1978.

Operating Manual for Spaceship Earth, by Buckminster Fuller. NY: EP Dutton, 1978.

Secrets of the Soil, by Peter Tompkins and Christopher Bird. NY: Harper and Row, 1989.

365 Outdoor Activities You Can Do With Your Child, by Steve and Ruth Bennett. Holbrook, MA: Bob Adams, Inc. Publishers, 1993.

holism

Holism and Evolution, by Jan C. Smuts. Highland, NY: The Gestalt Journal Press, 1996.

Holistic Management: A New Framework for Decision-Making, by Allan Savory with Jody Butterfield. Washington DC: Island Press, 1999.

> Written by the co-founders of Holistic Management International. It is *the* definitive, very readable explanation of Holistic Management practice and its evolution.

finances

Living More with Less, by Doris Janzen Longacre. Herald Press, 1980.

> Personal testimonies of families trying to simplify their lives. Offers suggestions on living with less.

Making Cents: Every Kid's Guide to Money, by Elizabeth Wilkinson. NY: Little Brown and Co., 1989.

> Stories and examples of different businesses kids have started and what you need to start your own.

Money Matters For Parents and their Kids, by Ron and Judy Blue. Nashville, TN: Oliver-Nelson Publishers, 1988.

Your Money or Your Life: Transforming Your Relationship with Money and Achieving Financial Independence, by Joe Dominguez and Vicki Robin. Penguin, 1993.

> This book has helped many people turn their financial attitude and situation around.

The Tightwad Gazette, by Amy Dacyzyn. NY: Villard Books, 1993.

> Lots of helpful hints for cutting expenses.

The Totally Awesome Money Book for Kids And Their Parents, by Adriane G. Berg. New Market Press, 1993.

> Discussions of planning, saving, earning, and goal setting

psychology

BrainStyles™: Change Your Life Without Changing Who You Are, by Marlane Miller. NY: Simon and Schuster, 1997.

Flow: The Psychology of Optimal Experience, by Mihaly Csikszentmihalyi. NY: Harper, 1991.

> Reviews research on the importance of having a vision beyond yourself.

From Stress to Strength, by Robert S. Eliot, MD. NY: Bantam, 1995.

> A good reminder for those who think that a stressful life is normal and won't hurt you.

Ishmael, by Daniel Quinn. NY: Bantam Books, 1995.

> Interesting novel about a gorilla that is a philosopher. Gets you thinking about why we do what we do.

It's All In Your Head, by Susan Barrett. Minnesota, MN: Free Spirit Publishing, 1992.

> A simple yet thoughtful book on how the brain functions.

Know How: Guided Programs For Inventing Your Own Best Future, by Leslie Cameron-Bandler, David Gordon, and Michael Lebeau. San Rafael, CA: Future Pace, Inc., 1985.

> Steps for building a life you want, based on observations of people who were successful in creating their own lives.

Live the Life You Love, by Barbara Sher. Delacorte Press, 1997.

> If you need to be encouraged to follow your dreams, this is the book for you.

Make the Most of Your Mind, by Tony Buzan. NY: Linden Press, 1984

> The man who brought us mind-mapping.

Mind Power, by Edward de Bono. London: Dorling Kindersley Limited, 1995.

The Path of Least Resistance: Learning to Become the Creative Force in Your Own Life, by Robert Fritz. NY: Fawcett Columbine, 1989.

Paradigms: The Business of Discovering the Future, by Joel Barker. NY: Harper-Collins, 1993.

Raising Your Emotional Intelligence, by Jeanne Segal, Ph.D. NY: Henry Holt and Company, 1997.

parenting

Seven Habits of Highly Effective Families, by Stephen Covey. NY: Golden Books, 1997.

> If you haven't read any of Covey's books on the "seven habits" then you might choose to read this one instead of his other books as it does offer exercises to help encourage those habits in all members of your family. Inspiring stories as well.

The Ten Greatest Gifts I Give My Children, by Steve Vannoy. NY: Simon and Schuster, 1994.

community, communication, and culture

The Art of Crossing Cultures, by Craig Storti. Intercultural Press, 1990.

The Different Drum: Community Making and Peace, by M. Scott Peck. NY: Simon and Schuster, 1987.

No More Teams!: Mastering the Dynamics of Creative Collaboration, by Michael Schrage. NY: Doubleday, 1995.

Rebuilding Community in America, by Ken Norwood and Kathleen Smith. Berkeley, CA: Shared Living Resource Center, 1995.

> Excellent book on discussing the possibility of all types of communities in all different kinds of locations.

For more information on Bob Chadwick's Consensus Building Process contact him at Consensus Associates, PO Box 235, Terrebonne, Oregon 97760, 503/548-7112.

management books anyone can use

The Fifth Discipline, by Peter Senge. NY: Doubleday, 1990.

The Fifth Discipline Fieldbook, by Peter Senge et al. NY: Doubleday, 1994.

Management of the Absurd, by Richard Farson. NY: Simon and Schuster, 1996.

> This is a good book to explore the paradoxes that affect our management or ability to work with people.

Typical daily water use for a family of four

Activity	Water use (gallons)
Toilet Flushing	100
Shower and bathing	80
Laundry	35
Dishwashing	15
Bathroom sink	8
Utility sink	5
Total	**243**

Source: U.S. Environmental Protection Agency (EPA)

Oftentimes we don't calculate the financial, social, and environmental costs of our natural resource use because we either think we need to have a lot more information than we really do or we feel overwhelmed by the task. But you can analyze your resource use in fairly simple ways to gain a general sense of your usage.

Resource use analysis is an important skill because of the relationship between environmental, financial and social costs. Consider how environmental costs (pollution and mining of limited resources to name two biggies) impact financial costs (most people have electric and water bills or must pay taxes for governmental use of those resources). In turn, these environmental and financial costs create social costs (health concerns for us or those affected by our resource use and financial stress on whoever is paying the energy/water bills). Below are water and electric usage calculation tables to help you begin calculating natural resource use. Of course, if you use propane for cooking and heating water or wood to heat your home, then you need to add those into your calculations. An excellent resource for exploring your natural resource usage is: *Save Our Planet* by Diane MacEachern, Dell Books, NY, 1990.

water use
calculation

electricity use
calculation

natural resource
inventory

water use calculation

See the table on the facing page for data from the U.S. Environmental Protection Agency (EPA) on the the typical daily water use for a family of four.

You can accurately calculate your water use by taking a gallon container, turning the tap on and seeing how long it takes to fill up that container. If it takes 15 seconds then you know you could fill four gallons in a minute which means your flow is four gallons per minute (GPM). So if you shower for 15 minutes you will use 60 gallons of water. However, if you put a low flow showerhead in your shower that regulates the water to 2 gpm, then your water usage would be 30 gallons. If you shorten your shower time to 10 minutes, you would use 20 gallons.

For toilets you can either check manufacturer's specifications or calculate the size of the tank. If you use a dam or some other way of displacing water (bricks or quart jars filled with water), then you would reduce your water use there multiplied by the number of flushes per day. To calculate your daily number of flushes, keep track for an average day.

For appliances like a dishwasher or washing machine you can check the manufacturer's specification. Older washing machines take more water than newer ones (unless you go back to a wringer washer).

For lawn and garden usage, you can use the same method of water calculation as mentioned earlier and multiply that figure by the number of hours you irrigate. Remember to fill the measuring container for calculation from the point where the water leaves your irrigation device as it may vary depending on the device you use. You can compare these figures against your water bill or a water meter that you can put in your home or on any water outlet or faucet.

electricity usage calculation

Most appliances have the wattage they use listed on them. However, some appliances list the volts and amps instead. If you multiple the volts by the amps you get the wattage. To calculate how much wattage you use on a given day for a particular appliance, multiply the wattage by the number of hours in use. You can then figure your total wattage by adding together the totals of all your appliances. If testing towards your holisticgoal indicates that a reduction of electrical use is important, you can purchase such energy saving devices as fluorescent light bulbs that can fit into incandescent sockets or energy efficient refrigerators.

If you want to calculate how these items add up, you can multiply your daily totals by 30 days to get monthly totals, or by 365 days to get yearly totals. In the example below, the difference between three incandescent light bulbs and three fluorescent light bulbs over the course of a year would be 246,375 watts and that's just for a small item. Imagine what your savings would be if your larger appliances were more energy efficient.

Electricity usage for various appliances

Appliance	Watts/hour	Appliance	Watts/hour
Refrigerator (runs approximately 14 hours/day)	490	Dishwasher	150
		Microwave (.8 to 1.5 cu. ft.)	1400
Freezer (runs approximately 14 hours/day)	750	Coffee pot (electric)	1200
		Food dehydrator	600
TV (25-inch color)	130	Range (small burner)	1250
TV (19-inch color)	60	Range (large burner)	200
TV (12-inch black and white)	15	Computer/Monitor/Modem	80
VCR	45	Ink jet printer	35
Stereo	15	Laser jet printer	1500
Cellular Telephone	24	Electric blanket	120
Fluorescent light (60W equivalent)	15	Table saw (2.0 hp)	2400
Incandescent 60W	60	Drill (1/8 hp)	300
Iron (electric)	1500		
Clothes washer	1450		
Furnace Fan	500		

This information was excerpted from Real Goods Solar Living Sourcebook. *For more information, contact Real Goods at 1-800-762-7325.*

Calculating electricity usage for your home

Appliance	Qty		Watts		Total watts		Hours per day		Daily total
Incandescent light	3	x	60	=	180	x	5	=	900
Fluorescent light	3	x	15	=	45	x	5	=	225
_____	_	x	___	=	___	x	___	=	___
_____	_	x	___	=	___	x	___	=	___
_____	_	x	___	=	___	x	___	=	___
_____	_	x	___	=	___	x	___	=	___
_____	_	x	___	=	___	x	___	=	___
_____	_	x	___	=	___	x	___	=	___
_____	_	x	___	=	___	x	___	=	___
_____	_	x	___	=	___	x	___	=	___

natural resource inventory

The following is a very simplified list of some of the typical items found in a home and the materials used to manufacture them. If you have difficulty doing the Natural Resource Inventory Exercise included with the other exercises in Appendix 1, this list will help you determine your natural resource use. There are other possible composites involved in the manufacturing of these products, and in many cases manufacturers use numerous chemicals in the production of various items. As this type of precision is not necessary for this exercise, I didn't include that information.

Item	Plant	Animal By-Product	Mineral
clothing	cotton	wool	polyester (petroleum)
shoes	rubber	leather	plastic (petroleum)
electronics			plastic and metal
windows			glass (sand and metal)
walls	wood		plasterboard (gypsum)
floor	wood		concrete
carpet	cotton	wool	synthetic (petroleum)
books/magazines	paper/wood		plastic
beds	cotton/wood		metal
dishes	paper/wood		plastic, ceramics (clay)
toys	paper/wood	fur, leather	synthetics

Other possible fiber sources are hemp (plant) or rayon (plant fibers treated chemically) or silk (animal by-product)

While more building products that are produced from plant waste are now available, in most conventionally built homes, the products used are either wood, a wood by-product (like plywood) or products manufactured from minerals (like ceiling tiles or linoleum).

Food can come from any of the categories listed above. Look at the labels on your food to determine if most of your food comes from the animal or plant families or if the manufacturer used many mineral or chemicals in either the processing of the food or the packaging. See if everyone in the house knows the origin of your food.

appendix 4

financial planning example

In the following sample sheets, I have created an Annual Income and Expense Plan for a fictitious family of Harry and Sue and their son, Hank. While the scenario is fictitious, it is based on real situations. Typically each column listed on the Annual Plan would have it's own worksheet. I have included only one sample income worksheet, one expense worksheet, and a sample control sheet for January.

In this scenario, Harry has a steady salaried job that provides the family with a take-home pay of $1885/month. Sue does contract work that offers more sporadic income which results in a yearly income of $6675 gross on which she must pay all taxes. As you can tell from the Annual Plan, they have accrued a substantial debt. They have already begun to address some of that debt by using Consumer Credit's services.

holisticgoal

When they set their temporary holisticgoal, this is what they wrote:

quality of life:

> We want clean food and water, good relations with friends and
> family, and a strong sense of community.
>
> We want to be debt-free and have financial independence.
>
> We want to do meaningful work and provide service to others.

forms of production:

> We will produce profit through work that fulfills us.
>
> We will acquire the skills we need to do the work that we want
> to do.
>
> We will produce a plan of action for community service.
>
> We will produce balance in our lives to have time for friends
> and family.
>
> We will produce a warm and friendly environment for ourselves,
> our friends, and our families.
>
> We will make decisions that insure that clean food and water are
> available to us.

future resource base:

> We will need to be perceived as honest, thoughtful, responsible, and community-oriented.
>
> We need to be connected with and participate in a community that values those qualities.
>
> We need to have community services that fill our basic needs for safety and growth.
>
> We need to have access to clean food and water.

financial planning

When doing their financial plan, they decided that the logjam was their debtload, which they would have to reduce to move forward.

While their gross profit was what they expected, they decided to increase Sue's income by adding an additional enterprise in the slower months of her current work. Because her slower time was in the summer when people needed to have other activities for their children to do, she decided to begin advertising her services for providing childcare during those months.

The weak link in this enterprise was product conversion. Sue needed to gain more skills to be able to earn a higher income. As a family, they decided that they wanted to invest in Sue this year.

You can see what they allocated in their first round of expense allocation on the current plan. In this plan they have not included any wealth-generating expenses to address their weak link. Instead they have chosen to wait. Once they actually attain their planned profit of $1200, they will invest it in classes for Sue. However, they would also like to make more payments toward their debt to reduce it. So, they will go back to look at how they can reduce some of their expenses to increase their profit and put some toward their debtload as well as toward Sue's training, which would require 100% allocation.

After looking at their expenses, they decided that they could get childcare for $150/month instead of the $217. They also decided that their cellphone service wasn't essential. Furthermore, they reduced their monthly communication costs to $45/month. Lastly, they decided to take a different medical plan that covered only major medical with a high deductible but only cost $90/month. With these changes they were able to increase their profit another $193/month which meant that at the end of the year they could pay off two of their loans, which would increase their profit an additional $200/month the following year.

These are all decisions they tested toward their holisticgoal. While they will have to watch their plan closely and not buy as many "fun" things as they have in the past, their plan shows them that they will have more profit in the next three years as they move out from under their debt. In that way, they will have more options with discretionary funds at the end of those three years.

EXPENSE WORKSHEET

4/29/99 13:44

Annual Plan Sheet Column Reference: Car maintanence

Seasonal Year -->		January	February	March	April	May	June	July	August	September	October	November	December	Item Totals:
Car loan	Plan	$300	$300	$300	$300	$300	$300	$300	$300	$300	$300	$300	$300	3600
	Actual													0
Oil Changes	Plan	$20		$20	$20		$20		$20	$20		$20	$20	160
	Actual													0
Tune-up	Plan									$100				100
	Actual													0
Tires	Plan					$250								250
	Actual													0
Timing Belt	Plan									$300				300
	Actual													0
Plan Totals:		$320	300	320	320	550	320	300	320	720	300	320	320	4410
Actual Totals:		0	0	0	0	0	0	0	0	0	0	0	0	0

appendix 4: financial planning example

Period / Type	Sue (Income)	Harry (Income)	TOTAL INCOME	Planned Profit (Exp)	Car maintenance loan (Exp)	Car Main and Loan (Exp)	CCCS Loan Harry (Exp)	Bank Loan (Exp)	CCCS Loan Sue (Exp)	Gas Credit (Exp)
Initial Balances, Rates, etc.>	675	1,885	2,560	200	320	370	100	100	310	110
January Plan	675	1,885	2,560	200	320	370	100	100	310	110
– Actual	675	1,885	2,560	100	320	320	100	100	310	130
Difference				100		50				(20)
Cumulative Difference To Date				100		50				(20)
February Plan	675	1,885	2,560	200	300	370	100	100	310	110
– Actual	675	1,885	2,560	200	300	300	100	100	310	110
Difference						70				
Cumulative Difference To Date				100		120				(20)
March Plan	675	1,885	2,560	200	320	370	100	100	310	110
– Actual	675	1,885	2,560	200	318	320	100	100	310	110
Difference					2	50				
Cumulative Difference To Date				100	2	170				(20)
April Plan	675	1,885	2,560	200	320	370	100	100	310	110
– Actual	675	1,885	2,560	200	300	320	100	100	310	110
Difference					20	50				
Cumulative Difference To Date				100	22	220				(20)
May Plan	675	1,885	2,560	200	550	370	100	100	310	110
– Actual	675	1,885	2,560	200	520	550	100	100	310	110
Difference					30	(180)				
Cumulative Difference To Date				100	52	40				(20)
June Plan	200	1,885	2,085	200	320	370	100	100	310	110
– Actual	200	1,885	2,085	200	300	320	10	100	310	110
Difference					20	50	90			
Cumulative Difference To Date				100	72	90	90			(20)
July Plan	200	1,885	2,085	200	300	370	100	100	310	110
– Actual	200	1,885	2,085	100	318	300	10	100	310	110
Difference				100	(18)	70	90			
Cumulative Difference To Date				200	54	160	180			(20)
August Plan	200	1,885	2,085	200	320	370	100	100	310	110
– Actual	200	1,885	2,085	100	300	320	100	100	310	110
Difference				100	20	50				
Cumulative Difference To Date				300	74	210	180			(20)
September Plan	675	1,885	2,560	200	720	370	100	100	310	110
– Actual	675	1,885	2,560	100	694	700	100	100	310	110
Difference				100	26	(330)				
Cumulative Difference To Date				400	100	(120)	180			(20)
October Plan	675	1,885	2,560	200	300	370	100	100	310	110
– Actual	675	1,885	2,560	200	300	300	100	100	310	110
Difference						70				
Cumulative Difference To Date				400		(50)	180			(20)
November Plan	675	1,885	2,560	200	320	370	100	100	310	110
– Actual	675	1,885	2,560	200	319	320	100	100	310	110
Difference					1	50				
Cumulative Difference To Date				400	101		180			(20)
December Plan	675	1,885	2,560	200	320	370	100	100	310	110
– Actual	675	1,885	2,560	200	319	320	100	100	310	110
Difference					1	50				
Cumulative Difference To Date				400	102		180			(20)
PLAN TOTALS	6,675	22,620	29,295	2,400	4,410	4,440	1,200	1,200	3,720	1,320
ACTUAL TOTALS	6,675	22,620	29,295	2,000	4,308	4,390	1,020	1,200	3,720	1,340

appendix 4: financial planning example

Period	Row	Sears at 21%	GE Credit 20%	Phone and Postage	Preschool	Utilities	Recreation and Misc	Food and Vitamins	Medical Insurance	Retirement	Pets	Rent	Auto Insurance	TOTAL EXPENSES
		Expense	Expense	Expense	Expense	Expense	Expense	Expense	Expense	Expense	Expense	Expense	Expense	Plan/Act/Diff/Cum
1	Plan	40	40	45	150	55	30	275	90	70	55	180	70	2,500
1	Act	40	40	75	150	75	30	350	90	70	55	180	70	2,495
1	Diff			(30)		(20)		(75)						5
1	Cum			(30)		(20)		(75)						5
2	Plan	40	40	45	150	55	30	275	90	70	55	180	70	2,500
2	Act	40	40	40	150	50	35	270	90	70	60	180	70	2,425
2	Diff			5		5	(5)	5			(5)			75
2	Cum			(25)		(15)	(5)	(70)			(5)			80
3	Plan	40	40	45	150	55	30	275	90	70	55	180	70	2,500
3	Act	40	40	40	150	50	25	270	90	70	50	180	70	2,425
3	Diff			5		5	5	5			5			75
3	Cum			(20)		(10)		(65)			5			155
4	Plan	40	40	45	150	55	30	275	90	70	55	180	70	2,500
4	Act	40	40	40	150	50	30	270	90	70	55	180	70	2,430
4	Diff			5		5		5						70
4	Cum			(15)		(5)		(60)						225
5	Plan	40	40	45	150	55	30	275	90	70	55	180	70	2,500
5	Act	40	40	40	150	50	35	270	90	70	55	180	70	2,665
5	Diff			5		5	(5)	5						(165)
5	Cum			(10)		0		(55)						60
6	Plan	40	40	45	150	55	30	275	90	70	55	180	70	2,500
6	Act	40	40	40	150	50	30	270	90	70	55	180	70	2,350
6	Diff			5		5		5						150
6	Cum			(5)		5		(50)						210
7	Plan	40	40	45	150	55	30	275	90	70	55	180	70	2,500
7	Act	40	40	40	150	50	30	300	90	70	55	180	70	2,255
7	Diff			5		5		(25)						245
7	Cum			0		10		(75)						455
8	Plan	40	40	45	150	55	30	275	90	70	55	180	70	2,500
8	Act	40	40	45	150	50	35	250	90	70	55	180	70	2,325
8	Diff					5	(5)	25						175
8	Cum			0		15		(50)						630
9	Plan	40	40	45	150	55	30	275	90	70	55	180	70	2,500
9	Act	40	40	50	150	50	30	300	90	70	55	180	70	2,700
9	Diff			(5)		5		(25)						(200)
9	Cum			(5)		20		(75)						430
10	Plan	40	40	45	150	55	30	275	90	70	55	180	70	2,500
10	Act	40	40	45	150	45	30	250	90	70	55	180	70	2,395
10	Diff					10		25						105
10	Cum			(5)		30		(50)						535
11	Plan	40	40	45	150	55	30	275	90	70	55	180	70	2,500
11	Act	40	40	40	150	65	30	275	90	70	55	180	70	2,455
11	Diff			5		(10)								45
11	Cum					20		(25)						580
12	Plan	40	40	45	150	55	30	275	90	70	55	180	70	2,500
12	Act	40	40	45	150	65	30	275	90	70	55	180	70	2,460
12	Diff					(10)								40
12	Cum					10								620
Total	Plan	480	480	540	1,800	660	360	3,300	1,080	840	660	2,160	840	30,000
Total	Act/Cum	480	480	540	1,800	650	360	3,300	1,080	840	660	2,160	840	29,380

	+/- (Deficit)	Bank Balance	Bank Interest Owed	Loan Payments	Loan Balance	Loan Interest Owed
Plan	60	60				
Act	65	65				
Diff	5	5				
Cum	5					
Plan	60	120				
Act	135	200				
Diff	75	80				
Cum	80					
Plan	60	180				
Act	135	335				
Diff	75	155				
Cum	155					
Plan	60	240				
Act	130	465				
Diff	70	225				
Cum	225					
Plan	60	300				
Act	(105)	360				
Diff	(165)	60				
Cum	60					
Plan	(415)	(115)				
Act	(265)	95				
Diff	150	210				
Cum	210					
Plan	(415)	(530)				
Act	(170)	(75)				
Diff	245	455				
Cum	455					
Plan	(415)	(945)				
Act	(240)	(315)				
Diff	175	630				
Cum	630					
Plan	60	(885)				
Act	(140)	(455)				
Diff	(200)	430				
Cum	430					
Plan	60	(825)				
Act	165	(290)				
Diff	105	535				
Cum	535					
Plan	60	(765)				
Act	105	(185)				
Diff	45	580				
Cum	580					
Plan	60	(705)				
Act	100	(85)				
Diff	40	620				
Cum	620					
	(705)	(705)				
	(85)	(85)				

Center for Holistic Management

4/29/99 14:53
Name:

CONTROL SHEET
For Month of: January

Sheet #:

Plan Column	Amount Adverse to Date	Cause of Deviation from Plan	Proposed Action to Return to Plan	ACT
Gas Credit	-20	Extra trips to town	Invite people here. Reduce extra-curricular activities. Car pool more.	H and S
Phone and Postage	-30	Made too many long distance calls	Write letters or email. Let other people call. Set phone dates and limit calls	S
Utilities	-20	Heat on too high. Colder weather than expected.	Dress warmer inside. Lower thermostat. Reduce water (electric for pump) and light usage.	H and S
Food and Vitamins	-75	Eating out too much. Buying luxury items	Buy more staples. No eating out until we get back in line.	H and S

gross profit analysis

	enterprise a			enterprise b		
	poor	average	good	poor	average	good
# items sold	200	200	200	500	500	500
price/item	**30**	**550**	**75**	**10**	**25**	**35**
total income	$6000	$10,000	$15,000	$5,000	$12,500	$17,500
materials	400	400	400	1000	1000	1000
advertising	300	300	300	250	250	250
transporting to market	—	—	—	2000	2000	2000
annual payments (capital interests on loan)	1000	1000	1000	1500	1500	1500
total expenses	1700	1700	1700	4750	4750	4750
gross profit	$4,300	$8,300	$13,300	$250	$7,750	$12,750

appendix 5

blank forms

Use of the forms

The forms in this section can also be ordered in enlarged format from Holistic Management International by

- calling (505) 842-5252
- mailing the request to 1010 Tijeras NW, Albuquerque NM 87102
- ordering through our web page at <www.holisticmanagement.org>
- or emailing <hmi@holisticmanagement.org>.

financial worksheet

annual income and expense plan

control street

EXPENSE WORKSHEET

4/29/99 15:48

Annual Plan Sheet Column Reference: 0

Seasonal Year-->	January	February	March	April	May	June	July	August	September	October	November	December	Item Totals:
Plan													
Actual													0
Plan													
Actual													0
Plan													
Actual													0
Plan Totals:	0	0	0	0	0	0	0	0	0	0	0	0	0
Actual Totals:	0	0	0	0	0	0	0	0	0	0	0	0	0

HOLISTIC MANAGEMENT

ANNUAL INCOME AND EXPENSE PLAN

	I1	I2	Income	TOTAL INCOME		E1	E2	E3	E4	E5	E6
	Income	Income	Income			Expense	Expense	Expense	Expense	Expense	Expense

Initial Balances, Rates, etc.>

January
- Plan
- Actual
- Difference
- Cumulative Difference To Date

February
- Plan
- Actual
- Difference
- Cumulative Difference To Date

March
- Plan
- Actual
- Difference
- Cumulative Difference To Date

April
- Plan
- Actual
- Difference
- Cumulative Difference To Date

May
- Plan
- Actual
- Difference
- Cumulative Difference To Date

June
- Plan
- Actual
- Difference
- Cumulative Difference To Date

July
- Plan
- Actual
- Difference
- Cumulative Difference To Date

August
- Plan
- Actual
- Difference
- Cumulative Difference To Date

September
- Plan
- Actual
- Difference
- Cumulative Difference To Date

October
- Plan
- Actual
- Difference
- Cumulative Difference To Date

November
- Plan
- Actual
- Difference
- Cumulative Difference To Date

December
- Plan
- Actual
- Difference
- Cumulative Difference To Date

PLAN TOTALS

ACTUAL TOTALS

(Per-month column entries: Plan, Actl, Diff, Cum)

E7	E8	E9	E10	Expense	TOTAL EXPENSES		+/- (Deficit)	Bank Balance	Bank Interest Owed	Loan Payments	Loan Balance	Loan Interest Owed
Expense	Expense	Expense	Expense	Expense		Plan						
						Act						
						Diff						
						Cum						

CONTROL SHEET

Center for Holistic Resource

Name: _____ Date: _____ Sheet #: _____

Plan Column #	Amount Adverse to Date	Cause of Deviation from Plan	Proposed Action to Return to Plan	ACT